SET YOURSELF *Free*

Copyright © 1999 by Sandra L. Krauss
All rights reserved, including the right of reproduction
in whole or in part in any form.

ISBN 0-9673198-0-3
Library of Congress Catalog Card Number 99-96609

Published by:
Success Talks Publishing, a division of Success Talks, Inc.

Designed by:
Autumn Lew • Graphic Minion Studios • Tulsa, Oklahoma

Manufactured in the United States of America
10   9   8   7   6   5   4   3   2   1

How to Order
Single copies may be ordered from Success Talks Publishing, P.O. Box 33593, North Royalton, Ohio 44133-3593; telephone 440-237-0777. Quantity discounts are also available. On your letterhead, include information concerning the intended use of the books and the number of books you wish to purchase.

SET YOURSELF Free

HOW TO UNLOCK THE GREATNESS WITHIN YOU!

Sandy Krauss

Dedicated to

*L*ady, the Messenger

I Set Myself Free

Words and music by Dale Gonyea

Today looks just like any day
But it's not any day
Today's the day
I finally found the courage to give my life a lift
Now everything's much clearer
Since I gave myself this gift.

I set myself free,
I set myself free
Free to be, the best me I can be
I set myself free, I set myself free
Since I stepped out of my way
There's no stopping me.

As I move forward, one thing is clear
The only thing that matters is right here.
I'm diving into life
From an exhilarating height
And refusing to be held back by a little thing called fright
Growing taller, branching out
Like the strongest tree
I set myself free.

Watch me grow,
Watch me grow
I learned so much the moment I let go
Watch me grow, watch me grow
The truth is all I ever wanted to know
And all at once my eyes got back their spark

I have no trouble glowing in the dark
And all the stumbling blocks
That held me back came tumbling down
I am lighter than I've ever been
And two feet off the ground
I'm filling up with love and I let it overflow
Watch me grow.

    Just breathing in and breathing out
Got me on the track and I found myself along the way
       And it's good to have me back
    And I will conquer any obstacle somehow
    And the most important time is happening now
    And giving up the fight was an incredible release
And for the first time in my life, I feel a total inner peace
      I'm moving forward, getting better
      Growing stronger and loving more
          Making changes
          Taking chances
       I will open every door
Getting closer every minute to the person that is me...

       I set myself free,
       I set myself free
       Now I am free.
       Yes, I am free
       I am free
       Oh, I am free.

TABLE OF CONTENTS

Preface vii

Acknowledgments ix

Chapter 1   How Did I Get Here Anyway? 1

Chapter 2   Saying Goodbye to Yesterday 17

Chapter 3   Learning to Love Yourself 29

Chapter 4   The Power of Positive Self-Talk 47

Chapter 5   Celebrating YOU! 57

Chapter 6   Creating Your Future 69

Chapter 7   How to Plan for What You Really Want 79

Chapter 8   Believe It — Then See It 93

Chapter 9   Never Give Up 105

Chapter 10 Celebrating Your Journey 115

Special Section 123
30 Techniques for Building High Self-Esteem

Recommended Reading 161

the adventure awaits...

PREFACE

A Japanese legend tells us that many years ago in the central part of Japan there was a mountain with a flat top surrounded by dense jungle. According to the legend, the mountain was called The Place Where You Leave Your Parents. If one's parents reached a certain age and they were still alive, their children carried them, bodily, through the jungle up to the top of this mountain and left them there for the gods.

One day there was seen a strapping young man, fighting his way through the underbrush, toward the mountain, carrying on his strong shoulders a tiny, frail old woman. As he fought and pushed his way through the jungle, heading for the mountain, the young man noticed that the old woman was doing something with her hands. He finally turned and looked up at her, half in anger and guilt at what he was doing and he asked, "Mother, what are you doing?"

The old woman looked down at her son, tears streaming down her wrinkled cheeks. She said, "Son, I'm just breaking off a few branches and dropping them to mark a path so that after you leave me, you will be able to find your way back home."

This book is about breaking a few branches for you. I haven't grabbed all the branches, and I'm still working on making my way through the jungle. What I do know is that in recent years as I have been working my way through the jungle we call Life, I have gained some wisdom and knowledge that has made a tremendous impact on me. And that's what I want to share with you.

I believe the ability to Unlock the Greatness Within You is in each and every one of us. We all have what it takes to accomplish goals, dreams and successes—usually beyond what we dreamed possible.

I hope you will find that wisdom in this book. Know that I do not have all the answers. What I do have is the passion to share with you what has made a tremendous difference in my life with the hope that it will do the same for you.

And now, get ready to

Set Yourself Free!

ACKNOWLEDGMENTS

This part of the book was probably the most difficult for me to write! As an avid reader, I remember thinking if I ever write a book, whom exactly would I include in my acknowledgments? This is a much harder task than you might ever imagine. I certainly wanted to include everyone who ever had or who is an influence in my life. That would take pages and you probably wouldn't read it anyway!

I finally decided that I would just take a deep breath and do my best. I trust that those who are not included would know they are important to me even though they might not see their name.

To my husband Ted, for his unending patience and love of me. To my parents, Bill and Laverne, to my sisters Kathy and Debbie and my brother, Bill and to their families: Don, Kendra, Jennifer and Bryan, Terry, Vicki, Katie and Alex.

I would like to thank the following friends and colleagues who have supported me on *this* project, either knowingly or unknowingly especially Rebecca Jacobson, Harrah Brown, Mike Grogan, Mary Ellen Klinc, Tom Krause, Lila Larson, Donna Hanson, Larry and Denise Seith, Mavis Allred, Nigel Risner, Susan Aldrich, Tim Zaun, Harold Usher, Thom Collier, Tony Tramontelli, Daniel Margaca, Judie Sinclair, Kate Zawodni, Edna Smith, Jim Van Bochove,

Tom Marron, Shane Murray, Sue Lionti, Laura Trzeciak, Julie Petras, Marilyn Warzecha, Barb Anderson, Linda Joseph, Larry Huffman, Jim Zaranec, George Malasca, Tracee Zubic, and my entire Facilitating Skills Seminar (FSS) family. Thank you for believing in me.

And a special thanks to Barbara Muller-Ackerman, who saw a vision in me and cared enough to hold me accountable to make my dream come true! This book would still be just in my head and on the computer if it were not for her gentle nudging and guidance along the way.

And most especially to Jack Canfield, the man whose work, wisdom and love I credit for setting me free and guiding me into the heights of abundant joy, success and blessings. Thank you, Jack.

SET YOURSELF *Free*

CHAPTER ONE

How Did I Get Here Anyway?

> *This time, like all times, is a very good one, if we but know what to do with it.*
>
> Ralph Waldo Emerson

CHAPTER ONE

ecause we haven't actually met, I don't know how old you are. You might be 22, 42 or 62. Or a wonderful age in between. That's not important. What is important is that by reading this book, you have decided to take the first step, or another step, to improve your life. I applaud you!

Be glad that you have made a decision to make positive changes in your life. You might feel a bit frightened, or overwhelmed or downright petrified! But let me tell you right now, it's worth it. In order to set yourself free, you need to understand the chains that bind you.

In all areas of our lives — intellectual, emotional, professional, and spiritual — the process of personal growth and development is the key to our success. When we believe in ourselves and really accept ourselves on the inside, we can be the master of our outer world. Our thoughts and the way we perceive our lives create our outcomes. What we think about, comes about. If we think success, we create success. If we think

how did i get here anyway?

failure, we create failure. What we need, to get the results in life that we want, is already inside us. The key is finding that vital belief in ourselves. It does not matter where or when we were born, what education we have, where we live or what is in our past. What matters is how we think about ourselves. If we want to change who we are, then we need to change the way we think we are.   There is nothing limited about our potential. Everything we need is already inside of us.

So if this is really true, why are we not living the lives we want? How is it that we have ideas and goals and dreams within us, yet each day we face the challenges of feeling we are nowhere close to being the person we want to be? Let's take a look at how our thoughts about ourselves are created.

Imagine yourself standing in front of the giant window of a maternity ward at your local hospital. Behind the window are several newborns, all unique in their tiny bodies. They all have different shapes; they all are different sizes; some are boys; some are girls.

Each of us was once a baby who left the hospital and went home with our primary caregiver, in most cases, our own parents. But no matter who took you home, they probably had little training for their job as parents.

Think about the education you have. Thousands of dollars were spent on teaching us how to read, how to write, how to find Europe on a map. But in my 16 years of formal education,

I never had a class, or the option of taking a class, that would teach me how to be an effective parent. Local hospitals and adult education programs may offer a class here or there, but the reality is, the art of being a nurturing, effective parent is left to chance. Most people raise their children using the same methods with which they were raised. Sometimes these methods are effective and most often they are not.

We rely, almost without hesitation, on the medical and educational communities to teach us and guide us on our children's physical and intellectual growth. Yet, where do parents have to go for guidance on raising children with emotional health? I think that even when parents see symptoms of low self-worth or emotional imbalance, they may refuse to seek professional help or the wisdom of a psychologist, often for fear of labels that might be put upon their children, or even themselves. I once saw these words on a church sign: "A parent's life is a child's guidebook." Many parents, I believe, have turned that around to read, "a child's life is a parent's guidebook." In other words, they are using their experiences from their childhood to guide them in their parenting. This is fine and acceptable if they had a healthy childhood. If not, the outcome can be devastating.

As infants, we all came into this world with perfectly innocent minds and thoughts. As healthy children, we are born with the potential to succeed. We are born with the potential

how did i get here anyway?

to live a happy, vibrant, brilliant life. We are pure in spirit; our potential is unlimited.

Almost immediately, each of us as tiny babies is influenced by a variety of external experiences. As children, we will be introduced to the world of our senses — sight, sound, taste, hearing and touch — all the senses that will shape our world. And without us even realizing what is happening, our subconscious mind is being formed; our world as we will see it is being created without us being aware of what is happening.

Each experience we have as baby, toddler, pre-school child and beyond is locked into our subconscious mind. In the filing system of our minds, all of our thoughts, feelings and emotions are being stored. For many of us, the files created in our minds are created instantly with each experience. For many of us, it takes a long time to remove unnecessary files, to clean out those we do not need and reorganize those that may be of value to us.

The accumulation of these files as we go through our childhood will be the main determining factor in the strength of our self-esteem. Our self-esteem will determine whether or not we go through life as a functioning child and adult or as one who struggles awkwardly through life. The difference lies in a person's attitude toward oneself, or the degree of self-esteem.

What is self-esteem? Nathaniel Brandon, author, psychotherapist and pioneer in the field of self-esteem defines self-esteem simply as "the disposition to experience ourselves as being competent to cope with the basic challenges of life and as being worthy of happiness." Another definition, from Dorothy Corkille Briggs, in her book titled, *Your Child's Self-Esteem*, is *how a person feels about himself. It is his overall judgment of himself — how much he likes his particular person. High self-esteem is not a noisy conceit. It is a quiet sense of self-respect, a feeling of self-worth. When you have it deep inside, you're glad you're you. Conceit is but whitewash to cover low self-esteem. With high self-esteem you don't waste time and energy impressing others; you already know you have value.*

She goes on to say that *a child's judgment of himself influences the kinds of friends he chooses, how he gets along with others, the kind of person he marries, and how productive he will be. It affects his creativity, integrity, stability, and even whether he will be a leader or a follower. His feelings of self-worth form the core of his personality and determine the use he makes of his aptitudes and abilities. His attitude toward himself has a direct bearing on how he lives all parts of his life. In fact, self-esteem is the mainspring that slates every child for success or failure as a human being.*

And so we begin our lives and the development of ourselves. Which brings us to the present. A present that might not be what we thought life was about. And we look to the past to see how we got here.

how did i get here anyway?

Looking at our past can be an uncomfortable, even painful, experience. As very young children, we want to love and respect our parents or the adults that are our primary caregivers. And we do just that. We go through childhood learning to live our lives in a way that will please our parents or caregivers. We might find ourselves making choices that will satisfy those who are important to us. We might even make choices that affect the rest of our lives for these influential adults.

In some parts of my life, that's how it was for me. And then one day I realized that I had been living my life, not for me, but for the way the outside world thought I should.

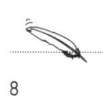

Here are some tough questions to ask yourself: Are you in a career that was chosen or suggested to you? Are you living in a certain city because you would feel guilty if you were farther away from your family? Are you in a relationship that isn't working, filled with fear when thinking about getting out?

I knew deep inside that there was more to life. I don't know exactly how I knew that. I just knew I wanted to feel different. I really believed my life could be better. I just didn't know where to start. I had concerns about how I would actually make the changes that I wanted to make. I found myself asking questions like what will happen to me, to my family, to those who are a part of my life? Will they accept the changes? Will they support me or criticize me? Let me assure you that these are very common questions and totally natural. Part of letting go is looking at what you know can be, the feeling inside that tells you there is more to life. Take a moment to love that feeling. Use the sensation to empower yourself.

Several years ago, I found myself filled with despair and frustration. I was once again looking at an overweight body in the mirror. I had tried every diet on the market, had joined and rejoined weight loss programs what seemed to be 20 times. I finally said to myself, "There must be more to life than losing and gaining weight and struggling every day to be thin. I need to find out why I cannot control my eating."

I had double trouble. Not only was I obsessed with food, I was obsessed with wanting a thin figure. I ate when I was happy, I ate when I was sad, angry, hurt, frustrated — you name it — food was my answer. Then I'd spend the rest of the day hating myself for not being able to control myself around food and for not having a perfect body. I thought for sure that there was really something wrong with me.

I discovered there was nothing wrong with me, just my thoughts about me! I found that what I lacked was love for myself. My self-esteem was really low. I had developed an unhealthy connection between my love of myself and the way I felt about my body. I was filling my mind with devastating self-talk, telling myself that I wasn't worthy of my love or anybody else's because I was overweight. I thought that's how the whole world thought — that people who are not attractively thin are not worthy of love, respect and support.

I learned to overcome this frail outlook on life! I started on my personal growth journey. And what I discovered was that the old adage, "It's not what's on the outside that counts, but what's on the inside" really is true. Inside I found a warm, caring, beautiful person, wanting to unfold in order to help others also see the beauty within themselves. I remember feeling odd at first with this newfound self. This new me was so much different from the person I had been living with for so long. I realized as I worked on bringing more of the new me forward, that I would never allow myself to return to my old patterns, my old belief system.

I also remember feeling a lot of confusion. I knew that I had waited a long time for a new me, and I found I wasn't sure what to do with her! That was when I realized that I needed to spend some time exploring just who I really was. It was exciting to know that with my newfound belief in myself, I could actually create more of what I really wanted in my life, and could learn to eliminate the old patterns that were not serving me.

If we really take the time to explore, we will find that many adults see themselves as less capable and lovable than they really are. We live in a world filled with negativity and forces that seem to be against us. It's easy to stay in our old patterns; it can be scary to reach out of our comfort zone and to take risks. Yet, if we choose to, we can create a today and tomorrow that is different from our yesterday. It does take courage, determination and a burning desire to succeed.

Oliver Wendell Holmes said, "What lies behind us and what lies before us are a tiny matter compared to what lies within us." Many of us do not even realize the potential that is already inside us, resources just waiting to be tapped. We are operating on only a small percentage of our capability! Think about the power our minds already possess. The power to think, imagine, decide, believe; the power of choice of learning, creating, loving, and of giving. And that is not the entire list. In order to become who we truly want to be, we need to live our lives with the understanding that we have no limits. Our potential is unlimited! I once saw a T-shirt that put it another way: No Limits, No Boundaries, Fired Up to Win!

For some, this way of thinking may be new. I suggest that you commit to putting aside some time for yourself every day to expand your "thinking horizon." The key is to really get to know yourself better. I find it very helpful to keep a journal. When I first started to keep a journal, it reminded me of my adolescent years of writing in my diary. A journal is like a diary for grown-ups! It is very much the same and serves much the same purpose. It allows us to capture and express our thoughts, ideas, feelings, fears, regrets, sorrows, accomplishments, sucesses, happiness — anything important to us at the time.

how did i get here anyway?

A journal not only allows us to release fears and frustrations; it allows us to have a conversation with ourselves. A journal is a way of clearing out the mental chatter that can hold us back. It can be scary if you have never kept a journal before. It may be the first time you ever really acknowledged your thoughts by putting them on paper.

You may need to give yourself permission to add this new tool to your toolbox of life. Spend time each day writing to yourself. My journal serves as a way for me to clear the cobwebs from my mind. I allow myself to just let the thoughts flow and I write them down. I tell myself that there are no rules. Spelling doesn't even count! Write down whatever thoughts come to your mind.

If you struggle with getting started, here are some questions you can ask yourself. You can use your journal to capture the answers.

- Who am I?
- What do I want?
- What makes me happy?
- What am I afraid of?
- What am I proud of?
- What is important to me?
- What do I want to accomplish in my life?

I suggest that as you are starting out, you use your journal on a daily basis. Make a commitment to spend time each day to reflect whatever it is you are feeling. The benefits of the journal are twofold: 1) you take the time to express your true feelings on a daily basis and 2) you have an opportunity to look back and to see how far you have come in your growth. You are able to reflect on your successes and triumphs, your accomplishments and the direction you are heading.

What does a journal look like? Your journal is whatever you want it to be. It might be a special gift you buy for yourself, with a beautiful floral cover or a geometric design that catches your eye. It might even be an inexpensive spiral notebook that you purchase at the local drug store for less than a dollar.

Another part of looking at ourselves more closely is to take a look at our attitude. It is our attitude that will drive us to success or failure, probably more than any other characteristic we possess. Bob Harris, in his tape program, "What's the Magnitude of Your Attitude?" poses the question, "Are you recycling inspiration or desperation?" What a great question! For many, we are so accustomed to our thought process that we never even stop to think of whether or not our perceptions are serving us or working against us. Just as we take care of our cars and have them checked regularly for peak performance, we need to do the same for ourselves.

Understanding how our thought patterns are developed and recognizing whether or not they serve us is the first step in making changes and setting ourselves free. Let's take a look now at why it's important to put the past behind us in order to make room for a magnificent today... and tomorrow.

Action Page - Chapter One

• *Changing Limiting Beliefs to Supporting Beliefs* •

The focus for Chapter One was to give you an opportunity to understand how your current belief system was developed. Take a moment to make a list of beliefs you have about yourself and your world that currently do not serve you. I call these limiting beliefs. Then recreate each belief as a supporting belief, one that will inspire and serve you. A few examples are listed to get you started.

My Limiting Belief	My Supporting Belief
• People over 40 are too old to change careers	❥ *I can be successful in a new career, regardless of my age*
• Having too much money is evil	❥ *I am worthy and entitled to abundance in my life*

_____   _____
_____   _____
_____   _____
_____   _____
_____   _____
_____   _____
_____   _____
_____   _____

how did i get here anyway?

CHAPTER TWO

Saying Goodbye to Yesterday

> *What spirit has done for others, can be done for you... when you're ready. The truth is, we're all chosen; most of us just forget to RSVP.*
>
> Sarah Ban Breathnach
> *Simple Abundance*

CHAPTER TWO

One of the biggest lessons I had to learn as I embarked on my journey is that you won't get far if you continually stop along the way and look over your shoulder. It's like trying to run a marathon with a ball and chain on your ankle.

I love the analogy Willie Jolley, motivational speaker and entertainer, uses. He reminds us that it's good to know about the past so you won't repeat the mistakes of the past. He says, unfortunately, some people get stuck in the past. They live in the past, dwell in the past, continue to talk about what happened years ago. Willie says, "the past is to be a place of reference, not a place of residence. There's a reason your car windshield is big and the rearview mirror is small. You're supposed to check behind you every now and then, but you're not supposed to dwell there." We know what happens if we do.

Releasing the past is probably one of the most difficult of all the steps necessary to set yourself free and unlock that greatness within you. For me, it was the most important as well.

saying goodbye to yesterday

As we go through life, we accumulate experience after experience. Every thought, picture and idea is stored within the great vastness of our minds. And for those of us who are fortunate, we enter a phase where we realize that life isn't working the way we expected it to. We agonize over careers that are less than satisfying, relationships that aren't working, health issues that weigh us down… day after day going by with unfulfilled dreams.

Have you ever wondered why what you really want hasn't come into your life? Most likely, it is because there isn't room for it. I use the analogy of a filing cabinet. If your filing cabinet is overstuffed with folders, papers and catalogs, there will come a point when you cannot possibly jam another piece of paper in there!

Our minds are the same way. If our heads and hearts are filled with experiences from the past and we refuse to let go, how can we expect anything new and better to enter?

The first step in saying goodbye to yesterday is to acknowledge and accept that you may have experiences from the past that have been hurtful, unpleasant or uncomfortable, realizing there needs to be a healing of these experiences. People won't change if they don't think there's anything in them that needs to be changed. Psychologists call that denial. And yes, I know, oh how I know, that the denial is so much safer, much more comfortable. But for many in denial, under the denial is the painful reality of a life unfulfilled. A life where we are dying a slow death. Each day, the pain eats at us, one disappointment, one heartbreak at a time. Before long, we experience depression, listlessness, a feeling of emptiness.

It is my belief that the best method for saying goodbye to yesterday can be different for each individual. Each person has different needs for releasing the past or letting go of patterns that may be holding us back, possibly even destroying us. After all, our past is our past and what it will take to release or heal it is up to us. I recommend that you explore an option that feels comfortable for you. A few I recommend are engaging in reading books, taking classes, attending conferences and workshops, joining a support group, counseling or therapy.

The options go beyond these. I used all of these myself, not at the same time, but over a course of years. The important point is that if you decide you might benefit from one of these avenues, be sure to take action on making it happen. If we were to study those individuals who are most satisfied with their current life experiences on a daily basis, one common thread I believe we would find is their commitment to heal and let go of their unpleasant yesterdays.

In courses on death and dying, those grieving are taught that in order to complete the grieving process a series of steps need to take place. The same is true for healing painful and hurtful experiences of our past.

For me, I found that working through these steps was most

effective when done with a trained professional. A trained professional will be able to help you work through the steps of healing: anger and resentment, hurt, fear, regret, expressing what you want, and finally love, compassion, forgiveness and appreciation.

Take some time to find a quiet, comfortable place and think about these steps. Ask yourself if there are situations in your past or even your present life that might need to be healed. If so, begin to explore avenues that feel comfortable to you for releasing what might be holding you back. You may know right away what is holding you back. I really didn't know what was keeping me chained up; I just knew that my life could be better. I had to go through a process, much like peeling an onion, layer by layer. Some layers were easier to get through than others. I refused to give up, even when I felt it was too painful to move on. I knew that for every layer of tough stuff I went through, I would receive the gift of feeling that I could conquer the world. The gift of joy and blessings.

Another part of saying goodbye to yesterday involves incompletions. What projects or tasks have you started that have not been completed?

Imagine that our minds are made up of attention units. I use the analogy of hangers in a clothes closet. If all the hangers are holding clothes and there are no extra hangers, we have no place for new clothes. Our minds work the same way. If we have incompletions in our lives, we are blocking new ideas and support from the outside.

Incompletions can include not choosing to even start a project, starting and never finishing, or leaving commitments with other people unresolved. Have you ever run into an old high school buddy and said, "Hey, let's get together for lunch sometime." "Sounds good," is the reply. Then you say, "I'll call you sometime." And the sometime never comes. Every time we think "I should call Karen for lunch," attention units are being used.

Our minds have many attention units, but they are not unlimited. Just as with our closets, every once in a while we need to clean out and make room for the new. This includes taking care of anything in our life that's broken, such as a dresser drawer, a frying pan handle, shoes, or that watch that needs a new battery. Every time we look at those items, it takes up energy. And that is energy that is not available for our current tasks at hand.

When I find myself with incompletions, I make the commitment to complete the tasks. Once completed, I always feel a renewed sense of energy. I feel a huge weight has been lifted off my shoulders.

My biggest struggle is with incompletions that deal with other people. I used to find it difficult to express my feelings. Although this is one area I am still working on improving, I am better at facing the fear head on. I always feel better when I do,

saying goodbye to yesterday

and often the relationship is stronger as a result of my actions. If I am not ready to approach the situation face to face, I write letters expressing what is on my mind. Sometimes I even write poetry. Most often, the letters never get mailed. Yet I feel a sense of relief. And the writing helps me to determine whether or not it would be best to confront the person openly and honestly. I often discover that the real issue goes beyond the surface to something that doesn't even have anything to do with the person I am struggling with. It's often an internal struggle within myself.

Now for the fun side of saying goodbye to yesterday! Yes, there are abundant experiences that we all have in our past that are worth celebrating. Celebrating our positive past helps us to realize the good that has taken place and to remind us of the greatness that once was and that can be.

There are many ways you can acknowledge your successes from the past. One is to divide your life into sections. You might do this based on the number of years you have lived. If you are 30 years old, you might have one section for the first 10 years of your life, the second ten and then the third. The next step is to make a list of as many positive experiences and accomplishments as you can from that time of your life. Your list might include recognition in grade school, a skill or talent you developed, a goal you set and achieved. The idea is to really focus on all the successes and celebrations of your past. You can later use these to provide the needed fuel to move forward to your goals and dreams.

Another idea for taking a look at the positive past is to make a list of positive categories. Your categories might include What I Am Proud Of, What I Have Accomplished, What Has Made Me Happy, and What Brings Me Joy. Then take time to bring forward favorable memories from your past and place them under one of the headings.

This can also be a lot of fun by making a picture collage of your successes. I once took a class in which one of our exercises was to sit among piles of magazines and cut out pictures or words or phrases that meant something to us. We then took cardboard pizza rounds, scissors and glue and created our collages. You can do both sides, punch a hole in it and hang it from your ceiling. One woman in the class said she and her daughter make collages all the time with different themes. She said her living room is filled with different expressions of herself.

Acknowledging the past is meant to be fun and exciting. You might simply just make a Gratitude List, with no rhyme or reason of what you are grateful for from your past. Displaying pictures, awards and symbols of your past accomplishments, successes and happiness will serve to remind you of what you are capable of doing.

Little by little, or in huge steps, by fixing and letting go of yesterday, and celebrating what we are proud of, we make room for the greatness of today and tomorrow.

saying goodbye to yesterday

Action Page - Chapter Two

• *Freeing Up Attention Units* •

In order to make room for abundance in our lives, we need to put order into our lives. This might include healing hurts from the past and dealing with incompletes.

Think about areas in your life that might be holding you back. Is there a relationship that needs to be healed? Do you find yourself among unfinished projects at home and at the office? Make a list of what needs to be completed in your life. Set a date for taking action to make this happen.

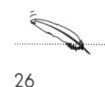

Incomplete Tasks	Action Date
(Examples)	
Put two years of vacation pictures into photo album	*June 18*
Have lunch with Rebecca	*March 31*
Resolve disagreement with Joe	*May 25*
_____	_____
_____	_____
_____	_____
_____	_____

INCOMPLETE TASKS	ACTION DATE

saying goodbye to yesterday

CHAPTER THREE

Learning to Love Yourself

> *It is not easy to find happiness in ourselves, and it is not possible to find it elsewhere.*
>
> Agnes Repplier
> *The Treasure Chest*

CHAPTER THREE

I find it amazing that for so long I found it so easy to love others before myself. I seemed to thrive on looking for ways that I could be of help. Someone would call me on the telephone, and I would have their request filled within the hour. I would spend hours at my desk writing cards and notes, sending cartoons across the country to anyone I met along the way.

Finally, one day it hit me. I said to myself, "Sandy, if you would spend as much time making yourself happy as trying to make others happy, you would probably be much closer to your dreams, much happier with yourself and much more productive!"

From a young age we are taught to be nice to other people — our siblings, the neighbors, people in the grocery store. Somewhere, though, many of us miss the connection that it is equally important to be nice to ourselves. We're often taught that if we like ourselves too much, other people might not like us. We might even be labeled conceited or arrogant. The truth is that in order to really care about other people on a genuine level, we must find the good in ourselves and care about ourselves. I say to parents in my workshops, "The wisdom in being a successful parent is not in what we give to our children, but in what we give to ourselves — first." What I mean by this is that we must first be certain that our own needs are met before we work on meeting the needs of our families, co-workers and friends. Unless we are taking care of our own needs and creating happiness for ourselves, it will be difficult to share true happiness with others.

This concept can be applied to any part of our life: the wisdom in being a successful partner, the wisdom in being a successful employee, the wisdom in being a successful friend. Its about finding a balance between what we need for ourselves and what we need for effective relationships in our lives, whether those are relationships at home, at work or at play.

In Chapter One, we talked about self-esteem in children. As adults, we might change our view of what it means to have self-esteem. Susanna McMahon, in her book *The Portable Therapist*, says,

> *There are many definitions of self-esteem, and what they all have in common is the concept of feeling good about yourself. This translates into loving yourself, respecting yourself, putting yourself first, and making sure your needs are met. Self-esteem means holding yourself in very high regard so*

that you not only love yourself, but that you act lovingly toward yourself all the time. The best way to think of self-esteem is to imagine that you love someone very much, that you are always pleased to see them and to talk with them, that spending time with this person is what you most want to be doing, that you think of them lovingly and try to do things to please them. Your beloved is the most important person in the world to you, and you will do anything and everything so that they know this. Now put yourself in the role of the beloved and act exactly the same way to yourself. This is self-esteem.

How do we develop love for ourselves? First, we need to let go of the need of telling ourselves how wrong everything is about us. Next, is to take a look at our environment. I'm not talking about your house, your car or your workplace, although those environments are important to our self-esteem. I'm talking about people. Whom do you spend your time with? Make a list of ten people you spend the most time with, at home, work or play. Then take a moment to think about the first person on your list. Is this person a loving, nurturing person — someone who supports you and lifts your spirit? Or is this a person who drags your spirit down, tells you why your ideas won't work and maybe even criticizes you?

Ask yourself these questions for each person on your list. Remember, what we think about, we create. If we are spending a lot of time with people who are less than loving, nurturing and supportive to us, we may find it hard for ourselves to be loving, nurturing and supportive of us.

After you've completed your list, you may want to re-evaluate whom you spend your time with. If you find that there is no one left on your list, celebrate, and start a new list! In other words, go out and find a new set of friends, a new career or position, new relationships. Or you may discover that you need to heal your current relationships.

When I did this exercise for the first time, I found I had only two people on my list that I could label as nurturing. Only two! That clearly showed me that I was spending my time with the wrong people. I have not totally eliminated these people from my life; I am just more selective about how much time I spend with them and more aware of the quality of our time together. Because our environment plays such a vital role in our success, we want to be certain we are creating a healthy environment for ourselves.

Another way to start to love yourself is to say to yourself, "I love you!" Does that sound silly? Think about it. How do your children know that you love them? How does your spouse know that you love him or her? Do you have friends that you care about? How do they know? It is usually because we tell them or show them! We need to tell ourselves and show ourselves too!

One of the best ways to do this is an exercise called the Mirror Exercise. I learned it from Jack Canfield, one of the world's leading experts in the field of self-esteem and peak performance. This is how it works:

Each night before you go to bed, stand in front of a mirror. Take a few moments to tell yourself what you appreciate about yourself from that day. You might include accomplishments, challenges you overcame, or steps you took toward your goals. Then before you walk away, look at yourself and say, "I love you." And hold eye contact.

Do not be alarmed if this is awkward at first. You may find yourself giggling, wanting to run or even feeling queasy. That's OK. Those funny feelings will go away as you continue. Do this for at least six weeks. You will start to see miracles in your life! I guarantee it!

When I committed to doing this, it was awkward for me at first. After all, I had never done anything like this before. But remember, I was committed to positive changes. So I would go to the mirror every night. The first time I did it, when I said, "And one more thing, Sandy, I love you," my response was "Yeah, right." But each day it got easier. One day I had received a compliment at work and I remember saying to myself, "I can't wait to get home to tell ME tonight!" I still go back to this exercise when I find myself at a low point or feel that I am struggling.

learning to love yourself

Another way to become more loving with yourself is to allow yourself the pleasure of touch. Virginia Satir, the late, noted family therapist, said there are four things we need in order to have high self-esteem: 1) to be listened to and HEARD, 2) to be attended to, especially through eye contact, 3) to have our relationships be equal, not one up and one down and 4) to be touched. She also believed that you need four hugs a day to survive, eight hugs a day for maintenance and twelve hugs a day for growth.

When was the last time you hugged your kids? Your spouse? How about your neighbor? A hug is a great way to let someone know that you care about them. No words need to be spoken. The message is clear: "You are special and loved." Take every opportunity to give your hugs away. You will receive so many more in return.

I never understood the power of touch until I attended an eight-day workshop in which we started each day with hugging. For me, it was awkward at first. Every day the hugs got easier. By the end of the week, I didn't want that part of the program to end. When I returned home, I could literally feel that my body was in hug withdrawal. I now ask for hugs when I need them.

One of the biggest steps toward a more loving relationship with yourself is to learn to ask for what you need. This was one of the hardest steps for me. After all, I thought that if people really cared about me, they would know what I wanted and needed.

We might go out of our way to acknowledge others, but when was that last time you gave yourself acknowledgment? Have you ever asked for a standing ovation? We all deserve one, just for being us! A standing ovation — oh, the roar of the crowd! Have you ever wondered how performers feel when the audience expresses its appreciation with a standing ovation? It's an exhilarating feeling to hear the thunderous applause and to see people standing on their feet acknowledging your accomplishment!

Why not experience the feeling yourself? You can get a standing ovation simply by letting people know you would like one. Tell your co-workers, family, fellow students, or anyone else in your life that you would like a standing ovation. Have them cheer and clap as loudly as they can for at least one minute. Take in the sight and sound of your very own standing ovation! Let it in. While you are receiving the ovation, watch the people who are giving the standing ovation to you and make eye contact with them. Feel the positive emotions that build up inside you and bask in the glory of it all!

Another way of loving ourselves is to take the time we need for ourselves. Every day, I talk to people who say they never seem to have the time they need for themselves. The result is feeling stressed, frustrated, and exhausted. Starting today, make

learning to love yourself

a promise to yourself that you will set aside at least 10-15 minutes each day to relax, reflect and refresh yourself. You might spend this time writing in your journal, meditating, taking a hot bath, or listening to music. It's your choice. Do what makes your heart sing.

I have a list of what I call my Life Enhancers, activities or people or places that make me happy. My list includes taking a walk in the park, spending time with family, talking on the telephone with my friend Rebecca, beaches and palm trees to name just a few. When I need to nurture myself and I'm just not certain what I need, I can look to my list and see what might bring joy to my life. Often we get into a trap of thinking that we are missing something grand — a new car, or a better job or more money. Actually, we often can find happiness within ourselves and in a simpler way.

If this is a challenging area for you, I highly recommend the book *Simple Abundance* by Sarah Ban Breathnach. Sarah's book is a gift to the world. Although it is written for women, men can benefit from it as well.

If it has been a long time since you have nurtured yourself, you might need a reminder as to what brings you joy. In addition to a Life Enhancer list, you might want to start a Picture Dream Book. The best way to do this is to look through magazines, old photo albums and picture books in search of images you are attracted to. Do you feel drawn to certain places, themes or people? Make a collage of whatever seems to stir emotions in you. You can then use your Picture Dream Book when you need to treat yourself.

I cannot over emphasize the importance of self-esteem, self-love and self-respect. Most psychologists and successful people agree that the way we feel about ourselves is the critical factor in our performance as human beings.

How much we like and respect ourselves affects every part of our performance cycle. For example, if you say to yourself, "I am terrible with remembering people's names," you create an image in your mind of meeting someone at the shopping mall and feeling embarrassed because you know you've met them and cannot remember who they are. Then you extend your hand and say apologetically, "I'm sorry, I don't remember your name. I'm terrible with names." The images that we hold in our minds will drive our outcome. In this case, you will want to change your image to you meeting people and remembering their names.

Once you understand this concept, the next step is to create a more positive *self*-image. We need to change the negative images of ourselves that we hold in our minds. Imagine that we have a scrapbook of photographs stored in that file cabinet in our head. We want to throw away the pictures with the failures, hurts and disappointments. Then we need to replace those pictures with photographs of success, happiness and

learning to love yourself

productivity. The images that we hold in our minds will either move us forward to take action or create a wall and keep us frozen and immobile.

Without high self-esteem, we will actually begin to self-destruct. We will break down emotionally and physically. What our mind possesses, our body expresses. What we think about ourselves on the inside shows on the outside.

This was especially true of Bunker Bean, the main character in a story written by Harry Leon Wilson and published in 1935. Bunker Bean was raised to believe he was a complete failure, inferior to everyone and everything. And he believed what he was told. All through his childhood and into adulthood, Bunker lived a life full of fear, cowardliness and defeat. One day Bunker Bean met a fortune teller and she told him that he was the afterlife of Napoleon Bonaparte. Bunker Bean, of course, was shocked to learn that he was once the master of the civilized world — rich, powerful and afraid of nothing. The fortune teller told him that he actually still possessed all of the qualities Napoleon had, and that the time was now right for those qualities to come forth in his life.

The amazing news inspired Bunker Bean. He spent hours in the library and hungrily read every book he could find about Napoleon. He collected pictures of the great emperor and hung them everywhere in his small, dilapidated apartment. He began to imitate the speech, manners and behavioral patterns of Napoleon. In his mind, he was becoming the great leader again.

Before long, Bunker Bean climbed to the top of the business and social worlds. He achieved wealth, power and fame. Then one day Bunker Bean discovered that the fortune teller had been a fraud. He had been deceived. He was not really the afterlife of Napoleon Bonaparte.

At first, Bunker Bean was devastated, but then he realized that in the time he had assumed the role of Napoleon he had formed the habits of success — habits that Bunker couldn't change. Being successful was now as natural to him as being a failure had been before. Bunker Bean concluded that every person is born to be successful. Inspired by the right people, their self-image would soar.

Think about how this story might fit into your life. Are you assuming a role based on messages and images created years ago? Know that you, just like Bunker Bean, have the opportunity to be someone different than you are. Who is your Napoleon Bonaparte?

My friend Jay told me a story about the janitor at the bank where he worked. He said the janitor was unkempt, had no teeth, and kept to himself. Then one day the janitor had the opportunity to attend a program featuring a group of motivational speakers. The janitor believed what he heard. He put the principles of success into action. He woke up every morning,

learning to love yourself

affirming what he believed, that he could make changes, that he could be successful. And it happened.

One day he came to work, his uniform clean and pressed. Then he came to work with a set of teeth. And then he came to work in a limousine and quit his job! He went on to become a successful millionaire. The media heard of his success and his story was featured on television and in the newspapers. That's what it takes — the belief in ourselves. I believe, I believe, I believe....

Action Page - Chapter Three

Affirming Your Strengths

The focus of Chapter Three was to encourage you to find the strengths you already possess. To help you realize just how good you already are, look at the following list. Check those qualities and characteristics that you already possess. Make a list of additional qualities that you possess. Then add qualities and characteristics you would like to develop.

accepts advice	caring	disciplined
admires others	clean	doesn't give up
affectionate	committed	effective
amiable	communicates well	efficient
appreciative	compassionate	encourages others
articulate	considerate	fair
artistic	cooperative	frank
assertive	courteous	friendly
athletic	creative	funny
attractive	daring	generous
bright	dedicated	gets things done
brave	dependable	giving
businesslike	determined	goal oriented
calm	diligent	good cook

learning to love yourself

good dancer	kind	responsible
good friend	loving	risk taker
good leader	loyal	self-reliant
good listener	mathematical	self-confident
good neighbor	mechanical	self-respecting
good parent	motivates others	sense of humor
good singer	musical	sensible
good with details	observant	sensitive
good with words	orderly	spiritual
good with hands	organized	spontaneous
graceful	on time	straightforward
grateful	open	strong
happy	optimistic	team player
hard worker	patient	tolerant
healthy	peaceful	trusting
helpful	persevering	trustworthy
honest	physically fit	truthful
humorous	pleasant	understanding
independent	polite	unselfish
inspiring	positive attitude	visionary
intelligent	punctual	vivacious
joyful	quick learner	warm
keeps agreements	respectful	well-dressed

Other characteristics and qualities I am proud of:

_____
_____
_____
_____
_____
_____
_____

Characteristics and qualities I would like to develop:

_____
_____
_____
_____
_____
_____
_____
_____

learning to love yourself

CHAPTER FOUR

The Power of Positive Self-Talk

> *Great spirits have always encountered violent opposition from mediocre minds.*
>
> Albert Einstein

CHAPTER FOUR

He hasn't called me because I'm too fat. My boss thinks I'm incapable. No one will ever love me. I knew I should have worn a different suit. Do these statements sound familiar? Many of us, as young children, learned to put ourselves down. Unfortunately, you might be saying these self-degrading messages to yourself even as an adult. The result is that constantly saying lousy things to yourself will actually end up making you feel lousy. The exciting news is that we can train ourselves for positive self-talk and work to eliminate the negative self-talk. Talking to ourselves in a positive way is a skill that can be acquired, just like learning to walk or operate a computer.

In a single day, you could have as many as 50,000 thoughts. Many of those thoughts might not be kind words. Often we talk to ourselves as if someone were scolding us. We call this *negative self-talk*. We say things to ourselves like "you can't do that," or "that was a dumb thing to say." I know that a key to

the power of positive self-talk

my success is my self-talk, because I believe that our minds actually work very much like a computer.

I remember when computers first hit the market there was a phrase "garbage in equals garbage out." I understand my mind to work the same way. When I talk to myself in a loving, supporting, nurturing way, I have exceptional results. When I talk to myself and use my negative self-talk, I have results that are less than desirable.

Dr. Norman Vincent Peale, in his work titled *Thought Conditioners*, reminds us that our thoughts are the basic ingredients to our inner lives and our happiness. This is from the introduction of his booklet:

> *Since happiness and effectiveness depend upon the kinds of thoughts we think, it is absolutely impossible to be happy if we think unhappiness-producing thoughts. If you put into your mind thoughts of fear, you will get thoughts of fear out of your mind. Fill your mind with resentment thoughts and resentment attitude will emerge. And in neither case, of course, can you find happiness-inducing thoughts. Whatever the condition of your mind, thought-conditioning is so powerful that it can displace unhealthy thoughts. Indeed, displacement is the only way you can drive a thought from the mind.*

So how do we change our negative self-talk to positive self-talk? Here are two techniques that I learned from Jack

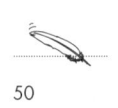

Canfield in his cassette program *How to Build High Self-Esteem*.

One of the easiest techniques was to first develop an awareness of using negative self-talk. For many of us, it is a habit we are not even aware of. When I find myself saying something that does not serve me, I say *cancel, cancel* and replace the negative self-talk with positive self-talk. If I found myself saying, "Sandy, that's a stupid idea," I would say *cancel, cancel* and restate my idea by saying "Sandy, you always have excellent ideas."

What can you do when your self-talk is generally positive, but you find yourself being judged by another person? In other words, what do you do when someone says to you "That's a stupid idea?" Jack Canfield teaches us to use the phrase, "No matter what you say or do to me, I am still a worthwhile person." This reminds me of the phrase I used as a child, "Sticks and stones can break my bones, but names can never hurt me." Both are powerful tools, no matter how you phrase them.

So the first step in combating negative self-talk is to develop an awareness of our own self-talk. I encourage you to really tune in to your own self-talk. Allow yourself to just notice when you use negative self-talk. After you become comfortable with recognizing your negative self-talk, begin to change the negative self-talk to positive self-talk. For many of us, if we have years and years of accumulated files in our mind containing self-defeating messages, it may take some time to replace

the power of positive self-talk

negative self-talk with positive self-talk that serves, inspires, and supports us. But it really works. Be patient with yourself.

I also surround myself with visual messages that remind me of the positives I want to create. I have posters and colorful cards that affirm what I want in my life. I have a T-shirt with "It Takes Courage to Grow Up and Be Who You Really Are" on the front. This is a vivid reminder for me to continue on my quest for authenticity and success!

If you like a challenge, practice your positive self-talk while looking at yourself in a mirror. Every day, spend one to two minutes with yourself. Talk to yourself as if you were encouraging a friend. After all, would you ever let friends get away with using messages that would set them up for failure? Say to yourself what you want to believe. Messages like "You can do it. You're doing a great job. You really worked hard today. You are fantastic. You are incredible."

Henry Ford said, *Whether you think you can or you think you can't, you're right.* A similar perspective is, *What you think about, comes about.*

Be gentle with yourself. At first, this may be awkward or even seem silly. Remember that the language you have developed with yourself has been in the making for several years. Changing your negative thoughts to positive thoughts will take time. It happens with a combination of being aware of your self-talk and spending time with people who believe in the power of positive focus.

Think positive for positive results. When you find yourself moving slowly and feeling unmotivated, pay attention to your thoughts. I would guess that your thoughts have had an impact on your lack of enthusiasm. Remember this simple phrase: *Positive Focus = Positive Results.*

Action Page - Chapter Four

• *Developing Positive Self-Talk* •

In Chapter Four, we focused on the power of positive self-talk. The best way to begin the process of changing our negative self-talk to positive self-talk that serves us is to begin to pay attention to what we say now.

For the next five days, each time you find yourself saying or thinking something that does not serve you, write it down. Then take a moment to think of a better way to focus on the outcome you desire.

Negative Self-Talk	Positive Self-Talk
You'll never finish this project	I am capable of succeeding at what is important to me
That was a stupid comment	I make good choices in what I say and do
You always forget your keys	I always remember my keys

Your list:

Negative Self-Talk	Positive Self-Talk
_____	_____
_____	_____
_____	_____
_____	_____
_____	_____
_____	_____
_____	_____
_____	_____
_____	_____
_____	_____
_____	_____
_____	_____
_____	_____
_____	_____
_____	_____
_____	_____
_____	_____
_____	_____
_____	_____
_____	_____
_____	_____

CHAPTER FIVE

Celebrating YOU!

> *The best way to see the good in others is to look for it in yourself.*
>
> Sandy Krauss

CHAPTER FIVE

*P*utting yourself first, really loving you, conflicts with what most of us have been taught. Our early childhood training emphasizes that it is better to give than to receive. Somehow the definition of share becomes misconstrued. Instead of following the dictionary definition of "to use, own, or receive jointly," we leave out the use and own part and look only at the jointly. We give to others before we give to ourselves.

Celebrating ourselves is rarely taught. Actually the opposite is usually what we learn. We have been taught that loving ourselves is selfish and that it will lead to becoming conceited. "People won't like you if you're conceited," gets translated into "If I like myself too much, I won't have any friends." On top of that we have been trained to believe our self-worth is dependent on how much we are liked by others. As you can see, it really ends up to be an unhealthy cycle.

To celebrate ourselves means to know ourselves. It means to recognize not only our weaknesses, but, more importantly,

celebrating YOU!

our strengths. Unfortunately, those strengths — or potential strengths — are often hidden beneath layers of self-doubt, perpetuated by messages from our outside world.

A 5-year old is scolded by her teacher for drawing outside the circle, or for coloring the tree trunk blue rather than "nature's" colors. This child may be more creative or experimental than others, but the message stored in the file cabinet in her mind is "I can't draw." Twenty years later, she finds herself unsatisfied in her career as an accountant because what she really wants to do is design work. Nobody knows us better than ourselves.

My message to you in this chapter is to find your true self. Who are you when no one else is around? How would you really dress, what would you really do for a career, who would you really spend time with, where would you really like to travel? These are all questions that can help you find the real you.

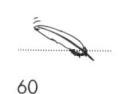

The biggest lesson for me in recent years has been the absolute necessity to find my authentic self. I know now that if I am not doing what is truly me, I am dissatisfied. For so many years, I was trying to be someone people would like, someone perfect, that I lost touch with who I really am. And I celebrated the day I discovered that even if I'm not perfect, people will like me anyway! I continue to celebrate my flaws, my weaknesses that make me who I really am. It feels good to know that I can be myself and not be a disappointment. And I also know that if someone doesn't like me, it just means someone doesn't like me. It doesn't mean that there is something wrong with me.

This was the discovery that inspired the title of the book. At the point in my life when I allowed myself to be me, I felt free. I felt I had broken the chains that had me bound and locked; unable to move forward.

I still face challenges in this area. I am still working on allowing myself to be even more authentic. The biggest challenge for me is to be vulnerable and to share thoughts and feelings with people I care about.

These situations get in the way of being authentic. Yet, as I continue to work on myself, and learn to love and accept myself the way I am, I know I will find the strength to create the relationships I really desire.

How do you discover your authentic self? Here are five important questions to ask yourself:

1. *What if it were only you?*

How would you live your life if you were the only one in your life? I know that might sound silly with over 5 billion people in the world. But give yourself permission to take some time to think about that question. If it were only you, what would you wear each day? What time would you get out of bed? What would you eat for breakfast? What kind of car would you drive? What time would you eat dinner? What would you watch on television?

Get the picture? I believe that many of us are living our day to day lives in someone else's picture. We dress a certain way because that's the company policy. We eat dinner at a certain time because our kids are hungry, even though we are not. I'm not saying that we should ignore the wants and needs of those who are important to us. What I am saying is that by answering these questions, we get a deeper sense of who we really are.

2. Whose comfort zone are you in?

The concept of "The Comfort Zone" was created by the late James W. Newman, the author of *Release Your Brakes*, and further expounded upon in 1998 in a book by Marilyn Sherman. When I saw the book and heard her speak, it hit me right in the face. What a powerful question. Whose comfort zone are you in? If you are not living your life the way you want to, why not? Some of us create our own comfort zones. Some of us allow others to create them for us. What do you do when you tell someone you are going to do something and they respond, "Oh, do you think that's a good idea?" If we change our mind, that's living in someone else's comfort zone.

My husband went with me to look for a storage cabinet for my office. We went into an office furniture store where the owner had some slightly used cabinets that had been used for just one weekend. They looked almost brand new. He said they would be $100 each. I thought that was a good price. I had done some shopping and hadn't found anything for less than that. Then I asked my husband for his opinion. He thought we should look around some more, and we left empty handed.

I continued to shop, never finding anything else for such a great price. When we returned to the same store, the cabinets were still there, but now they were $125. The owner denied quoting me a price of $100. At $125, they were still a good buy and I bought one, but I was angry at myself for not buying one the previous week, and I was angry at my husband for suggesting I continue to look.

The reality of it was, that my husband never told me not to buy it. I put myself in his comfort zone and adopted his perspective that it is not good to buy without shopping around — even when something looks like a good deal. I really had no right to be angry at my husband. If I had been my authentic self, I would have bought the cabinet the first time in the store. I knew the answer to "What would I do if it were only me?" would have been to buy the cabinet.

Take some time to explore the areas in your life where you may be feeling dissatisfied. Are you creating your own comfort zone or are you in someone else's? What can you do to move out of their zone and into an authentic place with yourself?

celebrating YOU!

3. What are your intentions?

This question gives us an opportunity to really look at what we do and why we do it. While discussing a business challenge with my friend Susan, I told her I wanted to help other speakers by starting a speakers bureau. This would help me in my speaking business and allow me to help others. That felt really good. Yet, when I had explored the details of operating a speakers bureau, I had realized there were a lot of avenues I had not considered. I was having doubts about whether this was a good business move for me.

Susan then said, "Ask yourself this: What are your intentions? Why do you feel you want to help these other speakers?"

It was the INTENTION part that got me. When I was really honest with myself, I realized I had gone into the venture with intentions that were not in line with my true self. I decided not to create the bureau, but to continue to help other speakers in other ways. When we act with intentions that are not in line with our authentic selves, we feel a struggle or a pull. We may find ourselves saying, "Something isn't right here."

4. What would you do today if you were brave?

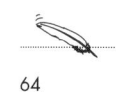

Wow! Doesn't that hit you between the eyes? It did me. This question will certainly help us identify our authenticity, do what we want, and go after our goals and dreams. That's what we would do today if we were brave. I now ask myself this question each day and do something to act upon what is important to me. If I had asked myself that question while shopping for the storage cabinet, I would have bought it. The answer would have been if I were brave I would buy this cabinet because I feel it is a good product for a good price. I would not have needed my husband's approval. Yet, it's those little seeds of self-doubt that sprout up and create weeds in our minds. Too many weeds make it difficult to see the real beauty of the lawn — the beauty of our goals and dreams.

5. What do I HAVE to have?

My friend Harrah was in a furniture store looking for a bed for her master bedroom. She was strolling along, paying attention to what she liked and what did not suit her taste when all of a sudden she saw it. The bed that she just had to have! Everything about it was perfect... except the price. No matter, Harrah had found precisely what she wanted and extended herself so she could buy the bed.

What do you have to have? Do you have possessions based on others' expectations? Do you live in a house that fits who you truly are? Does your decor match the real you? Are you driving the car you want, or did someone suggest to you that what you really wanted didn't fit your style or budget? Do you have to have recognition? Do you have to have success? Taking a look at what we have and what we want to have is a great tool

celebrating YOU!

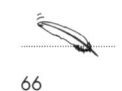

for exploring our authentic selves.

I found it so easy to stay in a trap of living my life the way I thought others wanted me to. I also found much of my pain and discomfort in this same place. It wasn't until I believed in me enough that I was able to begin the process of being me!

Teacher, speaker and author of *Touching Hearts ~ Teaching Greatness* Tom Krause says it nicely in the words of this poem.

Believe in Yourself
© 1999

If you dare to believe to follow your star
If you seek out your purpose to find out who you are
If you call on your courage to find hope in your heart
If you challenge your talent to fulfill its part
If love for your neighbor helps to shape who you are
If you still can have faith when you've traveled so far
If troubles and setbacks cannot stand in your way
If you find the resolve to live life every day
Then what you will find at the end of the road
Is strength of the heart and peace of the soul.

I encourage you to not underestimate the power of these pages. Discovering the real you is essential to Unlocking the Greatness Within You. After all, if you don't know who you really are, how will you know when the greatness has arrived?

Action Page - Chapter Five

• *Exploring Your Authentic Home* •

This exercise is designed to give you a chance to look further into the real you. Set aside at least an hour when you are home alone.

Take a walk through your home, including your basement and garage. As you stroll, pay attention to what you have — pictures, furniture, accessories, decorations. When you notice something, ask yourself where you got it, whether you like it, and why you have it. Think to yourself, "If I were brave today, would I keep this or discard it?" See if you can pull four or five items to donate to a charity. Spend time in your clothes closet and do the same. Let go of at least two outfits that you never feel good wearing anyway. I know they're in there! Let go of items you haven't worn for the last two years. Remember, as we clean out the old, we make room for the new. The new, authentic you!

celebrating YOU!

CHAPTER SIX

Creating Your Future

> *The future belongs to those who believe in the beauty of their dreams.*
>
> Eleanor Roosevelt

CHAPTER SIX

*Y*ou might be thinking to yourself that the ideas we've covered so far sound good in theory, but asking yourself if they really work. Yes they do. If you are able to read this book, the power of positive focus can work for you.

Remember when you were first learning to ride a bike? Didn't you at some point think you would never learn to ride without the training wheels? How about when you first learned to drive a car? Do you remember wondering if you would ever be able to parallel park, or merge onto a busy freeway? What gave us the ability to overcome those doubts? It was our desire and determination.

Do you know a 16-year-old in this country who does not want to learn to drive? Learning to drive is complicated. Beyond the laws, there are the skill aspects like maneuvering in traffic and braking on ice. But if we want something badly enough, we will learn what we must to get it.

I know that sounds simple, but if you didn't care about

creating your future

driving, you never would have learned how. You'd still be taking the bus or riding your bike to work.

So the first step in this process is to ask yourself what you want. If you could have anything, what would it be? Where would you live? Where would you work? What kind of car would you drive? Would you travel? If so, where to and with whom?

In order to set goals (covered in depth in the next chapter) you need to know what's important to you. This is often complicated by the clash between what we want and what we should want. What we want is a new red convertible. But because we have four children, we should want a mini-van. What we want is to teach physically challenged children. But our friends tell us we shouldn't want that because we can't make enough money in the field of education. When we face friction between what we want and what we should do or want, the result is confusion. When we find ourselves confused, we also find it easier to stay confused than to take action.

Okay, so here's the first step. Decide what you want. Let your imagination flow. Sit down with a pad and pen and write down everything you want to be, do or have. Dream big. For now, don't worry about the *how*. We're only looking at the *what*.

I once attended a seminar where we were given a homework assignment to make a list of *100 Things We Want to Have,*

Be or Do. It was fun, and it was highly enlightening. I incorporated my list into my book of goals.

If you have a difficult time developing your list, start this way. Ask yourself, if I could create my life exactly the way I want it, what would my (fill in the blank) look like? It would go like this:

- If I could create my life exactly the way I would want it, what would my job look like?
- How about the company I work for?
- If I could create my life exactly the way I would want it, what would my family be like?
- What would my house look like?
- Who would be my friends if this were a perfect world?
- If I could create my life exactly the way I would want it, what would my health be like?
- What hobbies would I have?
- What would my neighborhood look like?
- What about the world?

Many of us have decided that our lives are determined by outside forces so we may have never asked ourselves these kinds of questions. If we believe that we have control over our own destiny, these questions are crucial.

While you are doing this exercise, you might hear some voices inside your head—thoughts telling you that your wants are unrealistic. These are what I call members of the commit-

creating your future

tee. They are voices in our heads that bring with them a myriad of emotions and messages — messages that can serve us like, "You are courageous; go for it," and emotions like fear that keep us locked up.

It was my friend and coach, Mike, who first introduced me to the concept of *the committee*. The image made immediate sense to me and today I still will tell certain committee members to sit down and shut up! You may need to do the same while you are creating your wish list.

If we allow ourselves to bring forth the authentic self we talked about earlier, we will know what we want. It's the feeling that flows through us when we think about that trip to Australia, or a new home, or what it would be like to finish our degree. Use those senses to add to your list. After all, we aren't going to be able to reach all of our goals at once, and it's important to always have goals spurring our learning and growth.

Action Page - Chapter Six

• What Do I Want? •

Just in case you haven't embarked on this journey yet, here are starter pages for your 100 Things I Want to Do, Be or Have.

Remember, don't worry about the *how* for now. Dream big! Have fun! I've shared a few from my list to help get you started.

- Learn to ballroom dance
- Volunteer at hospital
- Take a cruise
- Be a guest on the *Oprah Winfrey* show

100 Things I Want to Do, Be or Have

1.
2.
3.
4.
5.
6.
7.
8.
9.
10.
11.
12.
13.
14.
15.
16.
17.
18.
19.
20.

creating your future

Set Yourself Free

21. ....
22. ....
23. ....
24. ....
25. ....
26. ....
27. ....
28. ....
29. ....
30. ....
31. ....
32. ....
33. ....
34. ....
35. ....
36. ....
37. ....
38. ....
39. ....
40. ....

41. ....
42. ....
43. ....
44. ....
45. ....
46. ....
47. ....
48. ....
49. ....
50. ....
51. ....
52. ....
53. ....
54. ....
55. ....
56. ....
57. ....
58. ....
59. ....
60. ....

61.	81.
62.	82.
63.	83.
64.	84.
65.	85.
66.	86.
67.	87.
68.	88.
69.	89.
70.	90.
71.	91.
72.	92.
73.	93.
74.	94.
75.	95.
76.	96.
77.	97.
78.	98.
79.	99.
80.	100.

Good job!

creating your future

CHAPTER SEVEN

How to Plan for What You Really Want

Having the world's best idea will do you no good unless you act on it. People who want milk shouldn't sit on a stool in the middle of a field in hopes that a cow will back up to them!

Curtis Grant

CHAPTER SEVEN

I remember when I first started learning about personal growth and development. One of the first concepts that became very clear to me was that the most successful people in life use goal setting. As a matter of fact, the first self-improvement audio tape program that I ever listened to focused exclusively on goal setting. It was six tapes dedicated to learning how to set goals and, more importantly, how to reach them. I was immediately excited about this concept, which was new to me.

As I listened to the tapes, I couldn't help but wonder why I had never set goals before. It didn't take me long to realize that the reason I hadn't was that I had never learned how! I didn't learn it in high school, I never took a course in college on goal setting, and up to that point in my business career, it had never been required. So the first step for me was simply learning how to set goals.

There surely are many different goal setting methods, so it is important to find a system that works for you. I also believe

how to plan for what you really want

that the goal setting system should be easy to use, should not require a lot of time, and should excite you so you will stick with it. Here are what I believe to be the most important elements of effective goal setting.

First, you must determine what it is that you want. I suggest that you take several hours, possibly even days, to think about what is most important to you — even though we all know what we want in general terms. For many of us, that includes good health, a satisfying career, a strong family unit, and financial stability. I believe it is vital to have balance in our lives and in our goals. For me, that means that I have balance in the areas of physical well-being, emotional well-being, relationships, career/finances and spiritual life. Let's take a look at each of these individually.

Physical well-being. Our bodies are the vehicle that we use to move us through our lives. In order to get the most from ourselves, it is important that we are physically healthy. This means proper nutrition and exercise. I am not claiming to be an expert or perfect in this area. Bad habits are hard to break. For me, the most beneficial changes I have made include less sugar and less fat in my diet and some type of exercise three to four times per week. I suggest that you determine what areas you need and want to improve. Make a list. And then decide which of those areas you will work on first.

My advice would be to start by making just one change. I

felt overwhelmed with all the changes I wanted to make until I decided to just focus on limiting the amount of sugar that I consumed. I then made a commitment to exercise at least three times per week. My exercise generally consists of brisk walking along with occasional bike riding, swimming, and backpacking. The key to your success is finding what you enjoy.

Emotional well-being. To have balance in your life, understanding emotions is essential. Many of us believe that emotions can be divided into good and bad, but I say emotions are simply feelings or reactions. I do believe it is important that we understand which emotions might serve us and which emotions might be getting in the way of our goals.

Understanding emotions can be complicated. My way of simplifying my own emotions, which I learned from Jack Canfield, is simply by telling myself that I have emotions, but that I am not my emotions. An example of this is that I might get angry, but being angry does not make me an angry person. When I feel angry, I ask myself where the anger is coming from. I allow myself to be angry and to know that releasing anger is healthy and necessary in order for me to move toward my destiny.

My friend Mike once shared an analogy that I have adopted when it comes to dealing with the emotions that are sometimes difficult to handle. He said that when various emotions surface, he pictures himself on the bank of a river, a gently rolling river. And when an uncomfortable emotion surfaces, he sees the emotion going down the river. For him, it's not about labeling the emotions, but just realizing they are a part of his life.

Relationships. We all need healthy relationships. This includes, but is not limited to, family, friends, co-workers, and neighbors. When I look back at the progress I have made, it is very clear to me how valuable my relationships are. I also understand that relationships change. Friends I had 20 years ago may no longer be a part of my life. I am also meeting new people every day. Take time to think about what is important to you in your relationships.

I used to think that what was important was the number of friends I had. What is important to me now is not the number, but the quality of the friendship. Ask yourself what you value about your relationships. Ask yourself if there are relationships in your life that could be enhanced or that should be eliminated. I learned years ago that some relationships enhance our lives and nurture us, and that some are toxic and take energy from us. My suggestion is that you begin healing or eliminating those relationships that do not serve you.

Career/finances. Millions of people do not enjoy their jobs. They find themselves frustrated, stressed, hopeless, and often victims of physical side effects. The connection between stress and wellness is a key reason that satisfaction in our careers is essential. After all, many of us spend the majority of our waking hours in our careers.

You may be going to a job every day that you do not enjoy because you believe you would not be able to make a living doing something you love. So you stay. I encourage you to at least explore other options if you are not satisfied.

Setting a goal related to what we truly want from our careers is one of the most important goals we can establish for ourselves... and it gets complicated by our financial needs. I used to believe that having a lot of money would be the answer. Now when I think about money and my finances, I think not only about what I need, but also about how I can share abundantly.

Spiritual Life. What is your spiritual life? I think spirituality is different for each person. For me, spirituality is a process—it's about expansion and growth. It includes love, truth, goodness, beauty, patience, giving and caring. It's what pushes us to move forward, to become focused. For many, spirituality provides a source of reality and most call that source God. I believe that it is our spirituality that gives us the guidance we need to move through life. It's a source of knowing that there is something greater than ourselves directing us on the path I call Life.

Sometimes goals appear too difficult to achieve. It is important to understand that when we set goals, we will often find obstacles in our way. An effective method for me to break down those obstacles is to clearly identify them. I take a piece of paper and write my goal at the top. Then I draw a series of blocks that represent bricks. This came from the feeling that I sometimes felt there was a brick wall in front of my goal. By writing on these bricks, I see obstacles that might get in my way. This also gives me the opportunity to break through those bricks.

What I found is that sometimes I would spend weeks working through one brick. Yet, other times two or three bricks would just seem to fall down effortlessly. Some of my bricks I still find myself chipping away at, even after several years.

Another illustration I use is writing my goal on a piece of paper with a mountain positioned in front of it. That mountain is made up of millions of pounds of earth. Some days I feel like I have a scooped away only a teaspoon of earth. Other days, I feel like I have attacked that mountain with a bulldozer! The point to remember is that no goal is too big.

If you completed the action page from Chapter Six, you already have a list of 100 things you want to be, do or have. And remember to think big. Small thoughts equal small results; big thoughts equal big results. You decide what you want. If you have not yet completed that exercise, please do so before reading on.

Let's start with just five items from your list of 100.

Five Things I Want to Be, Do or Have

1. _____

2. _____

3. _____

4. _____

5. _____

The next step is to make the goals clear. First, you want to state your goal in measurable terms. Ask yourself how you will know when you have reached that goal. For example, if your goal is to be wealthy, how do you define wealth? Would it be having $10,000 in the bank or $10 million? Remember, you determine what you need in order to fulfill that goal.

Next, determine a deadline for achieving your goal. Putting a completion date on your goal makes it more real to you and lets your subconscious mind know that you mean business. Having a time frame will also help you develop action steps for each part of your goal. Ask yourself, "By when do I want to have this in my life?"

Remember to think big, and yet to be realistic. It is not realistic for me to set a goal to complete the Boston Marathon next year when I haven't even had running shoes on for two weeks. Running a marathon requires dedication and tremendous physical conditioning for many months. A significant but more realistic goal might be entering a local 5-K (3.1 miles) run in the next half-year.

After you have specifically stated what you want and when, the next step is to decide how you will acknowledge yourself or celebrate when you have reached your goal. All too often, we work hard toward what we want and then do not take the time to congratulate ourselves and to reinforce our behavior when we accomplish what we had set out to do.

Now comes the time to break your goal down to specific action steps. Depending on the magnitude of your goal, you may have anywhere from one step to dozens, sometimes with mini-steps in between. Let's say your goal is getting an accounting degree. Before you can even start your education, you need to select a school, take entrance exams, apply to the school, and maybe take out a loan. Breaking your goal into steps will allow you to determine a plan of action. Ask yourself, can I complete this step today? If not, keep asking until you find an action you can take today. That way you are sure of working on your goal each day. Remember, success by the yard is hard; by the inch it's a cinch.

It is also important to express your goals in writing. Mark Victor Hansen, author and motivational speaker, says, "When you think it, ink it." Writing our goals on paper locks our ideas into our subconscious minds and alerts our minds to be on the lookout for resources that can help us reach our goals.

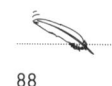

Sharing our goals with others can also help, but be careful with whom you share your goals. Be certain they are people who can support and encourage you and not those who will bring you down or set you up for failure. Many people feel threatened by the success of others and therefore may sabotage your enthusiasm for excitement.

Make a commitment to yourself to work on your goals each day. No matter what, find at least one mini-step you can take to move you closer to your objective.

Helen Keller put it nicely when she said "Life is either a daring adventure or nothing." Make your goal list an adventure.

Action Page - Chapter Seven

• *Setting Goals* •

Take time now, before we continue, to write at least three goals and the action steps required to reach each goal. Use the guidelines discussed in Chapter Seven.

The following worksheet can help guide you.

My Goal _____
_____
_____

Action Steps   By When?
_____
_____
_____
_____

Completion Date _____
Celebration _____

My Goal

Action Steps   By When?

Completion Date
Celebration

My Goal

Action Steps   By When?

Completion Date
Celebration

how to plan for what you really want

CHAPTER EIGHT

Believe It — Then See It

> *You ask for miracles - stand by.*
> *Understand that you will not be*
> *convinced even when you see them.*
> *When you change yourself -*
> *then you will be convinced.*
>
> Tim Piering

CHAPTER EIGHT

I feel compelled to start this chapter with some disturbing news. My news is that you can take what you learned in the preceding seven chapters and, if you do not believe you can do this, then that is the result you will get. Guaranteed! On the other hand, your life will be much more fulfilling if you focus on what you really want and not on what you don't want.

Because our minds are like computers, I think of the phrase *garbage in, garbage out*. Computer programmers the world over know that if you do not put the proper data into this wonderful machine, it will not give you the results you want. And our minds work much the same way.

Yes, I am saying it is as simple as that. What you think about comes about. And if we really believe that, we need to concentrate on what we want in our lives and not on what we don't want.

I AM are two of the most powerful words in our language. The next step in your success is to take your written goals and

believe it—then see it

turn them into "I am" affirmations. Affirmations are simply stating your goals as if they have already been achieved.

Let's use an example of a goal to learn a foreign language. Your goal statement might read "To enroll in French lessons and complete the course by December 31, 2000 or sooner." An affirmation would read, "I am happily and proudly speaking French fluently." Adding *sooner* or the words *or more* allows room for bigger and better opportunities to come into our lives and more quickly. Notice how the affirmation also includes feeling words, happily and proudly. The feeling words come from asking yourself how you expect to feel when each of your goals becomes reality. Be sure you use different feeling words for each of your affirmation statements.

Write your affirmations for each of your goals on a 3 x 5 index card. I use my affirmation cards the same way I used flash cards in grade school. Three times a day, I read the cards. I suggest you read your affirmations in the morning while your mind is fresh and open. Reading them again during the day helps to keep the energy going, reviewing them before you retire in the evening reinforces positive thoughts for sleep. Our minds actually replay while we sleep what we thought about before hitting the pillow so it's best that we fill our heads with healthy, supportive ideas. I suggest staying away from the evening news or violent movies before going to bed. Instead, fill your mind with uplifting thoughts.

Some people choose to write their affirmations on just one index card and carry that card with them wherever they go. This, too, is an effective tool. Find what method works best for you. I actually have both a set of cards and a single card I carry in my wallet. My affirmation cards are connected to my goals and more of what I want to do or have, while the card I carry in my wallet has affirmations for creating the person I want to *be*.

The following is a true story that clearly illustrates the power of believing in what we want and creating the visual aid to make it happen. *The Card* was written by Tom Krause and is featured in his book titled *Touching Hearts — Teaching Greatness*.

I remember how I felt when the idea hit me. Thrilled, and certain. Ready!

It was in algebra class, the spring of my junior year. Football season was long over, and the next season was a long time away. We'd done well last season - qualifying for the playoffs for the first time in school history - and I wanted us to do even better next year, my senior year. How? That's what was on my mind while Mr. Grimes was explaining infinity. Then the idea hit me.

I didn't wait till after school. During my lunch break, I drove over to a print shop and ordered business cards with a simple, direct prophesy - "BOONVILLE PIRATES — 1974 STATE CHAMPIONS!"

When the cards were printed, my teammates and I distrib-

believe it—then see it

uted them all over town. Teachers pinned them to classroom bulletin boards. Merchants taped them in store windows. Soon those cards were everywhere. We worked hard at getting the cards all over town. There was no escaping them, and that's what we wanted. We wanted our goal to be right in front of us, for all to see, impossible to overlook, no matter where we went.

When football practice started again in late August we were focused. That sense of direction and unity made us a closer team. From day one we gave more in practice, paid more attention to detail as we executed assignments sharply.

We had the goal imprinted in our minds, in our hearts — "BOONVILLE PIRATES — 1974 STATE CHAMPIONS!" We marched through the season undefeated and stepped into the playoffs with a sense of destiny.

The first playoff game matched us against a powerhouse team that was riding a 28-game winning streak. We knew we were in for a fight, but as the intensity of the game increased, so did our determination. We won, pulling away in the second half.

That win brought us to the brink of our goal, a match-up with the defending state champions for the title. We went into preparing for the big game with the same calm intensity and focus we'd shown as a team all season. Then it started to snow. A huge storm blew through stymieing everyone. School was canceled; roads were closed; transportation systems shut down. Still, somehow every member of the team made it to the school gym and we practiced for the biggest game of our lives in tennis shoes. We heard that the state officials were thinking of canceling the game and declaring the teams Co-champions. We continued with practice anyway. No way, we thought. This was our year.

On Saturday, we arrived at the stadium to find the field buried in snow. The goal posts seem to float on a cloud. Someone asked if snowshoes would be allowed as legal equipment.

"What I want you to remember," Coach Reagan said in the locker room before the game, "is that weather is fair to both sides. Both sides will tire of trudging through wet, heavy snow. Both sides will have trouble holding onto a wet, slippery ball. You're going to hate the conditions, but the game still turns on execution, on which team plays with better skills and more conviction."

Both teams struggled to a scoreless first half. In the locker room at half-time, Coach Reagan reminded us of all we had been through to get to this moment. "Remember your goal - Remember your focus - remember - THE CARD!"

Playing conditions were as tough the second half as they were the first, but our determination didn't numb out with our fingers and feet. We held in there, and pulled away in the second half again, scoring 34 points to their 14. Our year-long goal became fact: "BOONVILLE PIRATES — 1974 STATE CHAMPIONS!"

And yes, Tom still has his card!

Another way of affirming what we want in our lives can be expressed through pictures. Some of my affirmation cards

believe it—then see it

have pictures from magazines of places I want to go or things I want to have. I love to travel so I have an affirmation card with a picture of a cruise ship on it. Another card has a picture of a 5-star resort. And some of my cards have only written words describing what I want to create in my life.

Here are some example of some affirmation statements you may want to use to create what you want in your life.

I am healthy.

I am happy.

I am energetic.

I am successful.

I am helpful to myself and others.

I am resourceful.

I am sincere.

I am a good listener.

I am patient.

I am persistent.

I exercise daily.

I keep my commitments to myself and others.

I am organized.

I hope you get the picture. Basically, figure out what you want, write it down and add the words I AM to each statement. Affirmation statements should be short. Keeping them short also makes it easier for you to remember them and repeat them often.

Our minds react similarly to what is real and what we are imagining. That can be both good news and bad news. The bad news is that we often create unnecessary FEAR! The good news is that we can actually program ourselves to greatness.

Within our brains lies what is called a reticular activating system, located at the base of the spine. Everything that filters into our brain goes through this system. The reticular system decides what we pay attention to and what we ignore. If we didn't have that filter, we would be bombarded with information and images, far beyond what we are capable of handling. As powerful as our brains are, they are unable to concentrate on all the information at one time.

We can program our reticular system by our beliefs about ourselves, our self-image and our needs. If my self-image says that I dress poorly and then someone compliments my new outfit, I am likely to not trust their message. There's nothing in my system to validate their kind words.

By using affirmations and visualizing what we want, we are actually able to reprogram our system. We can reinforce our new self-image. We can program ourselves for what we want to pay attention to. We can create pictures of what we want to create in our lives. Create pictures for each of your goals. See them becoming real. Hear voices congratulating you on your accomplishment. Savor the feelings of joy and pride in your body. Program yourself for greatness today!

believe it—then see it

Action Page - Chapter Eight

• *Creating Affirmations* •

Just as we spent time writing goals at the end of Chapter Seven, we are now going to write Affirmations in order to create a new tomorrow. Remember that an affirmation is a positive statement you say to yourself as if the goal has already been achieved.

Guidelines for Affirmations:

1. Start with *I AM*.
2. State them in the positive and use present tense.
3. Keep them brief and specific.
4. Include feeling words, such as proudly, excitedly, or happily.
5. Repeat them three times a day, or more.

My Affirmation Statements:

I AM _____

I AM _____

I AM _____

I AM _____

I AM _____

I AM _____

I AM _____

I AM _____

Keep a copy of your affirmations with you. You many want to make several copies and keep one at home, one with you at work, even one in the car. I know people who tape record their affirmations and play the tape as they drive.

Remember that your mind reacts in a similar way to a real event and an imagined event. If you make a habit of programming your mind with these positive statements, the old negative messages will eventually lose their power and go away.

CHAPTER NINE

Never Give Up

> *Those who say
> it cannot be done
> should not interrupt
> the person doing it.*
>
> Chinese Proverb

CHAPTER NINE

*H*enry Wadsworth Longfellow once said, "Perseverance is a great element of success. If you only knock long enough and loud enough at the gate, you are sure to wake up somebody."

This chapter is about taking action! It's about doing! And it's about never giving up!

I hope setting goals and writing affirmations was enlightening and enjoyable. And if you were serious, it took some time. The next step is to keep this activity in motion.

Have you ever known someone who colors every conversations with all that he or she plans to do? And you start to notice a pattern. They are always talking about finding that new job, or remodeling the bathroom, or taking that trip to Hawaii, but none of those things seem to happen. After a while, you may find that you don't ask about what they've been up to because you know you'll get the same old song and dance.

I felt that myself, as I first worked on this book. It seemed nothing moved as fast as I had hoped. Whenever my friend

Shane asked, "How's the book," he got the same answer for almost a year.

"It's coming along," I'd reply. "Not as fast as I'd like, though." Shane must have wondered if he'd ever see it. Let's face it, people want results, not excuses or broken promises.

Finding the excitement to set and begin pursuing your goals may come easily. Maintaining that excitement takes time, energy and effort. And remember, a body in motion stays in motion. Your job is to find the motion and keep it going.

Probably the best way to keep the excitement, enthusiasm and energy going is to commit to doing something every day that will bring you closer to your goals. Involving yourself in activities that are in alignment with your goals, vision, and beliefs will keep you on track. This is also a great way to make decisions. Ask yourself the simple question *will doing this take me closer to or further away from what is important to me?*

Make a list of activities that you can and must do on a daily basis to move you toward your objectives. Develop habits or daily routines that move you forward. Be careful not to let yourself get stuck. It's easy to do if you are not aware of the activities you are spending time on. As you are starting on your journey, consider keeping a time log. This is an excellent way to get a clear picture of how you spend your time. Often we figure that it won't take much time to make that telephone call, or watch a little bit of television, or stop at the shopping mall. But doing small activities that are not in alignment with our bigger goals can be time wasters.

I'm not saying you should never make telephone calls, watch television or go to the mall. What I am suggesting is that you become aware of time allocated to activities that keep you from working on your goals. We all need time for relaxation. Be sure you build that into your daily and weekly activities. Just make certain recreation does not fill your weekly calendar unless you are on vacation! Balance is the key.

Know that there may come a time when you feel as if you have been working forever and you are still not where you want to be. Also know that obstacles are a part of our journey. Without obstacles, achievement would feel rather empty.

In their best-selling book series *Chicken Soup for the Soul®*, authors Jack Canfield and Mark Victor Hansen share a number of challenges some very well-known people have had to face. An expert once said of Vince Lombardi, "He possesses minimal football knowledge. Lacks motivation." Walt Disney was fired by a newspaper editor for lack of ideas and went bankrupt several times before he built Disneyland. Thomas Edison's teachers said he was too stupid to learn anything. And Babe Ruth, a legend for his home run ability, also held the record for striking out.

How different our world would be if these giants had quit

when the going got tough.

In the words of Dr. Benjamin Mays, "It must be borne in mind that the tragedy of life does not lie in not reaching your goal. The tragedy lies in not having a goal to reach for. It is not a calamity to die with dreams unfulfilled, but it is a calamity not to dream. It is not a disaster to be unable to capture your ideal, but it is a disaster to have no ideal to capture. It is not a disgrace not to reach the stars, but it is a disgrace to have no stars to reach for. Not failure, but low aim, is sin!"

Never let go of your goals.

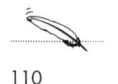

Action Page - Chapter Nine

• *A Daily Plan for Motivation* •

Probably the best way to stay motivated is to stay focused on your successes and accomplishments. All too often, we forget to acknowledge ourselves for what we have achieved. Take time each day to keep track of what you feel good about and what you are grateful for from that day. A journal is a great way to keep track of your progress and your insights.

1. What did I accomplish today that I am proud of?

   _____
   _____
   _____
   _____

2. Did I reach any of my goals today?

   _____
   _____
   _____
   _____

never give up

3. Did I take any risks today?
   What did I do today because I was brave?
   _____
   _____
   _____

4. Did I take action on anything I have been putting off for some time?
   _____
   _____
   _____

5. Did I take time to laugh and relax today?
   What made me happy?
   _____
   _____
   _____

6. How did I spend quality time with those I care about?
   _____
   _____
   _____

7. Did any pleasant surprises happen today?
   _____
   _____
   _____

8. Who did I acknowledge today for a job well done?

_____

_____

_____

9. Did anyone acknowledge me today?

_____

_____

_____

10. What did I do today to stay motivated?

_____

_____

_____

11. This is what I am most thankful for today.
    See if you can make a list of five.

    1. _____
    2. _____
    3. _____
    4. _____
    5. _____

never give up

CHAPTER TEN

Celebrating Your Journey

> *If one advances confidently in his dreams, and endeavors to live his life which he has imagined, he will meet success unexpected in common hours.*
>
> Henry David Thoreau

CHAPTER TEN

*D*id you ever spend several hours on a project for someone else and not receive the recognition you thought you deserved? I think all of us can remember a time when we felt an investment of our time or talents went unnoticed. Yet, most of us invest thousands of hours for ourselves and fail to give ourselves the recognition we deserve.

In order to continue our quest of personal excellence, we need to continually recognize and reward our efforts. So often we take ourselves for granted. When we are successful, we often pass it off as no big deal. Ask yourself, "If I treated my friends the way I do myself, would I have any?" We spend more time praising and recognizing the efforts of our friends, family members, and co-workers than we do ourselves.

Applauding yourself may feel awkward at first. You can begin tracking your successes and victories by writing them down in a notebook or on file cards. Some people prefer to collect symbols or trinkets that represent their successes. This part

celebrating your journey

of acknowledging ourselves can be fun. Let your creativity soar.

Think about what you enjoy most in life and write these down as your rewards. I called this my Life Enhancers list — things that make me happy. My list includes walking on the beach, spending time with my nieces and nephews, watching butterflies, and reading a good book. I refer to this list when I am looking for ways to acknowledge myself for what I have accomplished. What keeps me energized and motivated is knowing that when I accomplish what I set out to, I will be recognized. Even if it means recognizing myself!

We might call that patting ourselves on the back, but would we go to work day in and day out if we did not receive a paycheck at the end of the week? Some of us might. But most of us see our salary as the reward for a job well done. Ask yourself, what will my personal salary be for my efforts toward personal excellence? Here are a few ideas that might help you to celebrate:

- Do something just for you. Take yourself on a date.
- Keep a Victory Journal and add victories and glories to it each day.
- Spend time with people who inspire and support you.
- Treat yourself to a gift — especially something that isn't too practical.

Every day is an opportunity for growth. Every day can take you closer to your dreams, to Setting Yourself Free and Unlocking the Greatness Within You. I wish for you the best of success on your journey.

Stay Motivated!

Action Page - Chapter ten

• *Getting Ready for Action!* •

Congratulations! You made it! And you worked hard! Now you are ready to Set Yourself Free and Unlock the Greatness Within You. Before we end, take time to think about your next step, your action plan. What I want you to think about are ways to work around any obstacles that may occur and ways to celebrate your successes.

Obstacles That Might Occur	My Plan of Action
_____	_____
_____	_____
_____	_____
_____	_____
_____	_____
_____	_____
_____	_____
_____	_____
_____	_____
_____	_____

Ways for Me to Celebrate my Success!
My Life Enhancer List

celebrating your journey

SPECIAL SECTION

30 Techniques for Building High Self-Esteem

> *Life isn't about finding yourself.*
> *Life is about creating yourself.*
>
> George Bernard Shaw

SPECIAL SECTION

These are activities you can do on a daily basis to keep your spirits high and to keep feeling good about yourself.

I would like to acknowledge my dear friend Mary Ellen Klinc for working with me on developing these ideas.

#1
Start Each Day in a Positive Way!

Studies show that people who have something to look forward to will perform better and will have a more energetic outlook. Ask yourself every morning, "Today, what am I looking forward to?" It might be attending a sporting event that evening, dinner with friends, reading a good book near the fireplace. Identify a bright spot as you begin each day.

Remember...
Positive Focus = Positive Results!

#2
Get Your Daily Hugs

Virginia Satir, the late, noted family therapist, said we need four things to have high self-esteem: 1) to be listened to and heard, 2) to be attended to, especially through eye contact, 3) to have our relationships be equal, not one up and one down, and 4) to be touched. She also believed that you need four hugs a day to *survive*, eight hugs a day for *maintenance* and twelve hugs a day for *growth*.

When was the last time you hugged your kids? Your spouse? How about your neighbor? There is no better way to let someone know that you care than to reach out and give them a hug. No words need to be spoken; the message is clear: "You are special and loved." Don't miss the opportunity to give your hugs away. You will receive much more in return.

#3
Standing Ovation

Oh, the roar of the crowd! Have you ever wondered how the performers feel at the end of a great show when the audience expresses its appreciation by giving them a standing ovation? It is an exhilarating feeling to hear the thunderous applause and to see people standing on their feet acknowledging your accomplishment!

Why not experience the feeling yourself? You can get a standing ovation simply by letting people know you would like one. Tell your co-workers, family, fellow students, or others you trust that you would like a standing ovation. Have them cheer and clap as loudly as they can for at least one minute. Take in the sight and sound of your very own standing ovation! Do not hold back. While you are receiving the ovation, watch the people who are giving the standing ovation to you and make eye contact with them. Feel the positive emotions that build up inside you and bask in the glory of it all!

#4

An Apple a Day...

What if it really is true... That an apple a day does keep the doctor away?

The food we eat provides our body with the energy to work, play and rest, but our food choices sometimes might not be the best. The discipline and planning required to select nourishing food is well worth the effort when we find we have a higher energy level, maintain a healthy weight and feel better overall. Instead of feeling regret and finding yourself unhealthy because of poor food choices, why not enjoy the feeling of satisfaction knowing that you are taking good care of yourself? Go ahead, have an apple a day!

#5
Possibility Thinking

Do you look for reasons something cannot be done instead of searching for ways in which it can? Do you tend to demand a guarantee of success before you begin a project? Do you make decisions out of fear?

Be honest with yourself. If you answered *yes* to one or more of these questions, you might be suffering from impossibility thinking!

Create unlimited possibilities. Changing the way you think about yourself can change your performance. Look for the possibilities in your life!

Become a Possibility Thinker.

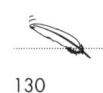

#6
Keep in Touch!

We are living in a time of mobility. Many of us no longer live in the same neighborhood in which we grew up, or have moved at least once or twice in our lifetime. As a result, we run the risk of losing contact with friends who are important in our lives. Studies show that people with strong relationships have lower mortality rates, but keeping in touch with those friends across the miles can be a challenge. Here are some ideas on sending love long-distance. Find the chance to keep in touch with someone you love and care about!

1. *Stay in touch via electronic mail.*
2. *Write a newsletter to all of your long-distance friends bringing them up to date on what is going on in your life.*
3. *Make an audio or a video tape so you can be seen and heard across the miles.*
4. *Send a postcard from a spot you once shared. It will bring back pleasant memories for both of you.*
5. *Send a "coupon book" for items that your long-distance friends can redeem such as one phone call from you a month, a weekend visit or a recent photo of yours truly!*

special section

#7
Avoid Toxic TV

Turn on the television set and chances are you will be hard-pressed to find something that is not laced with negative behavior and violence. Dramas, soap operas, and some evening programs fill us with scenes of murder, robbery, abuse and profanity in the name of entertainment. Ask yourself if this is what you want programming your mind.

There are worthwhile television programs, but they aren't always the heavily promoted programs on major networks. It is important to be discriminating in what messages you allow into your subconscious mind. Ask yourself if the program is one that uplifts and motivates or is one that is destructive and depressing. You would not put something into your body that you knew was harmful, so why would you choose to do that to your mind? Make good television choices.

#8
The Victory Wall

Take a large sheet of paper, preferably the length of the wall or door. Title it "My Victory Wall." Make it a fun project by using colorful markers. This paper is for acknowledging your victories and successes or sharing successes with each other. For example, you might write on the victory wall: I finished my taxes before April 15, or I organized the basement storage area, or the marketing department met their deadline. The idea is to focus on the positive activities and outcomes that you are proud of. If covering a wall or door seems to be too large, consider using a piece of poster board instead. This can be used in the office, at home, as well as in churches or by coaches and players in the locker room.

special section

#9
The Victory Log

This is the same concept as the Victory Wall except each person acts individually. You can use anything from an inexpensive spiral notebook to a beautiful leather-bound journal. Each day, write down all the positive activities and successes from that day in no particular order. List all actions, regardless of their significance. The following might be part of one's list:

- submitted report to manager on time
- practiced golf putt
- spent quality time with the kids
- took spouse to dinner
- exercised for 1/2 hour

Remember Positive Focus = Positive Results!

#10
Books, Books, Books

A wealth of knowledge is right at your fingertips. Your local library and bookstore are gold mines! Motivational books give you an opportunity to learn from the triumphs and challenges of others. Books can help you to grow, to learn and to educate others.

Of all the skills we gained while growing up, learning how to read has to be one of the greatest gifts. Use this gift to support and inspire you to your goals and dreams.

You can find books on every topic, including those areas of your life you have concerns about. Dedicate 30 minutes a day to reading, learning and exploring.

special section

#11
The Total Truth Letter

When we are upset, we often hold back our true feelings. Writing a Total Truth Letter can help release the emotions we may have bottled up inside. The next time you have an unresolved conflict with someone, write that person a letter. Write as much as it takes to address each of the following stages one needs to go through when resolving conflict:

1. Anger and Resentment: "I'm angry that..." or "I don't like it when..."
2. Hurt: "It hurt me when..." or "I feel disappointed about..."
3. Fear: "I was afraid that..."
4. Remorse, Regret and Accountability: "I'm sorry that..." or "I didn't mean to..."
5. Wants: "All I ever want(ed)..." or "I deserve..."
6. Love, Forgiveness, Compassion and Appreciation: "I understand that..." or "I forgive you for..." or "Thank you for..."

It would be ideal if both persons involved in the conflict would write a Total Truth Letter about the unresolved issue and share it with each other. However, **you will benefit from this process even if you do not share your letter with anyone.** You can even throw it away when you are done. It is critical that you identify your feelings and express them.

* I want to acknowledge Jack Canfield for teaching me this exercise.

#12

Keep a Warm and Fuzzy File

A warm and fuzzy file can be a valuable tool to help you develop your self-image and bolster your spirits on a down day. The file can be a folder, box, large envelope or any creative receptacle you devise. Use it to store letters and greeting cards, notes of acknowledgment, or small tokens of appreciation. Over time, you will be amazed at the treasure you have filed away.

Whenever you are feeling a bit down, go through your warm and fuzzy file and you will quickly be reminded about how special you are and the times you made a difference in someone else's life. And don't just wait for those more challenging days to go through your file. Make it a habit to review it on a regular basis. It can make a difference between a good day and a *great day!*

#13
Keep a Journal

A journal can be a powerful tool for keeping your self-esteem high. A journal gives you the opportunity to express your thoughts, feelings, fears, accomplishments, regrets, sorrows, successes — the possibilities are endless.

Your journal is whatever you want it to be. It might be a special gift you buy for yourself, with a beautiful floral cover or a geometric design that catches your eye. Or it might be an inexpensive spiral notebook that you purchase at the drug store for less than a dollar.

Be sure to use your journal on a daily basis. Make a commitment to spend a few minutes each day to reflect whatever it is you are feeling at the time. The benefits of the journal are twofold: 1) you take the time to express your true feelings on a daily basis and 2) you have an opportunity to look back to see how far you have come in your growth. You will be able to reflect on your successes and the direction you are heading!

#14
Volunteer — Give Back

Almost all successful people seem to have one common message they share: *Whatever you want more of, you need to give away.*

A sure path to achieving higher self-esteem is volunteering your time, talent or resources. Helping others helps us to feel good about ourselves. Volunteering creates a sense of accomplishment and self-worth. The success and stability of many organizations is dependent on having volunteers. Therefore, when we donate our time or talents, we feel needed.

If you want to have more time in your life, give time away. If you want more money in your life, give more money away. Add this rule of thumb to your daily living: *What I put out comes back to me.*

Be persistent. Be patient. You will be amazed at the miracles you can create in the lives of others and in your own life!

special section

#15
Notes of Acknowledgment

One of the greatest gifts you can give to another person is the gift of acknowledgment. ALL of us want and need to be appreciated. Taking the time to let others know what you appreciate about them can work miracles.

Here is an easy way to be certain that you stay on track with your acknowledgments: Set aside half an hour each week to spend time acknowledging those who have made a special contribution to your week. That might mean a brief note to a coworker for helping you with a project, a note to your teenage son thanking him for washing your car, or a telephone call to your grandmother just to tell her you are thinking of her.

So many times, we let these opportunities slip by until we think "It's too late." By scheduling a time each week to express these important sentiments, you'll be sure to say *Thank you, I appreciate you* or *You are special to me*.

#16
Take a Hike!

OK, you're reading it again. Physical activity is a critical element to our overall health and wellness. Even if your lifestyle is sedentary, you've probably said at least once, "I feel so much better when I'm exercising!"

Exercising does not have to be an unpleasant activity. The key to success is to find an activity that you truly enjoy. Then start to build this activity into your weekly routine. Keep on, one day at a time. Psychologists say it takes 28 days to change a habit.

While you are developing your new routine, watch your self-talk. If you are talking down to yourself while exercising or telling yourself how hard and uncomfortable it is, you are likely to give up. Find what you like and make it fun. Involve your family or friends.

If you have young children, why not give them a gift they can use for a lifetime? Make daily activity as much a part of their lives as brushing their teeth or eating dinner. They will grow up healthier and avoid the struggles so many adults have with incorporating exercise into their lives.

#17
Plan Your Future

Would you ever plan a driving trip across the country without using a road map? Living your life without plans and goals can result in an unplanned destination. Successful people use goal setting in one form or another to guide them to their success.

Goal setting does not have to be a scientific process. Simply take the time to think about what it is you want out of your life. Consider setting goals in the following areas to ensure a balance in your daily living: physical, emotional, relationships, career (includes financial) and spiritual.

Work on a few goals in each area. Be sure you write your goals on paper and look at them on a daily basis (some experts say three times a day). Share them with others so you can get support and encouragement. Be sure to affirm your goals by talking to yourself as if you have already achieved the goal. Use pictures whenever possible.

The late Earl Nightingale summed up goal setting by very simply saying: *People with goals succeed because they know where they are going.*

#18
Self-Stick Note Therapy

This fun, easy and inexpensive idea can help build self-esteem in every member of the family, including moms and dads. Leave random notes throughout the house and in lunch boxes, school bags or briefcases. Write messages like "I'm proud of you," "You can do it," "Keep up the good work," and "I love you."

One man shared the story of how he would leave notes throughout the house for his daughter. One day he went into her room to look for a tool he had misplaced. As he was leaving, the back of her door caught his eye. She had accumulated over 200 self-stick notes and was saving them on her door. He knew that when she left the house each day she was reminded her dad loves her! *

---

* Story taken from *How to Build High Self-Esteem* by Jack Canfield. Nightingale-Conant Corporation.

#19

Surround Yourself with Supportive People

To achieve your goals, you need to share them with others who will support you.

It's important to find a group of individuals who share similar dreams and goals. Join together and support each other! Chances are you will find many others who believe in your dreams.

Consider joining or starting a Master Mind group. A Master Mind group consists of two or more persons (two to six is ideal) who meet regularly in an atmosphere of trust and harmony for the purpose of providing mutual support and encouragement — and to believe for each other things which each, alone, may find difficult to conceive and believe.

#20

The Mirror Exercise

Believing in yourself and loving yourself is crucial for a lifetime of happiness and success.

Each night before you go to bed, stand before a mirror and take a few moments to tell yourself what you appreciate about yourself. You might include accomplishments from that day and challenges you overcame. Then before you walk away, look at yourself and say to yourself "I Love You." And hold eye contact. Do not be alarmed if this is awkward at first. You may find yourself giggling or wanting to run. That's OK. Those funny feelings will go away as you continue.

Do this for at least six weeks. You will start to see miracles in your life!

* I want to acknowledge Jack Canfield for teaching me this exercise.

special section

#21
Attend Seminars and Workshops

We are never too old to stop learning. A big part of success and happiness is to continue to learn and grow.

Find classes or programs that interest you. There are seminars and workshops on almost every topic imaginable.

This is also a great way to meet new friends or others who will support you. Chances are you will have a lot in common with the other participants. After all, you enrolled in the same program!

#22

Hang Around Positive People

What you think about comes about. If you are spending time with people who have a negative outlook on life, guess what? You most likely will develop that same dreary attitude.

On the other hand, if you surround yourself with people who are energetic and see situations in a positive light, you will tend to be more upbeat and optimistic. Rather than drain your energy with negative thoughts, conserve your energy for all that you want to accomplish.

special section

#23
Look for the Good in Others

To feel good about ourselves, we need to see the good in others. Our world is a miracle. Each of us makes a precious contribution to life as a whole. Make a commitment to start to look — and sometimes you really have to look — for the good in others.

To raise our self-esteem, we need to let go of judgment of others. Start by devoting one day to being non-judgmental of others. Notice how good it feels. Now try another, and then a week. Before you know it, rather than seeing what you do not like in people, you will be seeing what you really cherish about them!

#24
Strength Bombardment

Take a plain piece of paper and simply list several qualities that you like about a person. Write as many as you can think of. Don't hold back. You might list virtues such as patient, a good cook, honest, makes good decisions. If you were doing this with your children, you might include good ball player, pretty eyes, helps with baby brother, helps Dad with chores.

Then be sure to share the list! We often think that important people in our lives know what we like about them, but they won't unless we tell them!

special section

#25
Circle Talk

At least once a week, or more often if time allows, gather your family to sit in a circle. Pass an item, such as a soft cloth heart or a teddy bear. When you have the item, it is your turn to talk. You can talk about whatever you want. The others are to just listen. No comments are to be made. Let each person talk for a set time, depending on the size of the group. This exercise allows you and your children to express feelings, concerns, excitement, fears—whatever is important at that moment.

This exercise is also effective in work settings and in schools.

#26

Take on a Leadership Role

One of the best ways to develop confidence in ourselves is to serve others. In a leadership role, we have the opportunity to serve others and to develop new skills, enhance skills we already possess and teach others to develop their skills.

Learning comes from doing. In most organizations, especially community groups, leaders are given an opportunity to learn and grow with the help and support of fellow organization members. If you belong to an organization, think about becoming an officer or volunteering for a leadership role. Usually the commitment is for one year. At the end of that year, you will have a new set of experiences, successes and skills... and many good memories!

#27
Visit a Nursing Home

As we've said, one of the surest ways to build self-esteem is by helping others. Throughout your community, there are homes for the elderly filled with people who would love a visit from you. While many residents have frequent visits from their families, others do not. Think about taking a half hour, maybe once a month, to visit someone who would be delighted to receive the companionship of another human being.

You can look in your telephone directory for a list of homes. Call ahead to see if they have programs for volunteers who would like to visit their residents.

#28
Sing a Song

Don't cringe at this one! Even if you have never been in a choir or you have been asked to "keep it low" while singing in school or church, singing is good for the soul.

If you classify yourself as "tone impaired," don't fret. Nobody has to hear you. Sing in the shower; sing in your car; sing when no one is around! Consider going to a music store, buying the lyrics to one of your favorite songs and grabbing that imaginary microphone!

If you have a desire to sing publicly and do not feel comfortable with your voice, think about taking voice lessons. Yes, voices can actually be developed. If you wanted to play the piano, you would take piano lessons, so why not consider singing lessons? After all, your dreams don't have to be *Somewhere Over the Rainbow!*

#29
Take Yourself on a Date

Don't think there's a misprint here! Yes, taking yourself to a movie, dinner, or a Broadway show is totally acceptable. Feeling good about ourselves especially includes when we are alone.

Have you ever wanted to attend an event, but felt stymied because your partner or friends did not share the same enthusiasm? Why not plan a special evening just for yourself? You name the place, the time and the activity. And yes, you'll be delighted to pick up the tab!

#30
Become a Mentor or Coach

One of the greatest satisfactions we can experience comes from helping others. Each of us is good at something, and sharing that quality, skill, talent or training could enhance someone else's life. Why not spend time each week sharing your gift with a child, another adult or a group that could benefit? Remember, what we give away comes back to us. You will be rewarded many times for the time and talent you share with others.

EPILOGUE

Some Thoughts Before You Go...

> *You made it!*
> *CONGRATULATIONS!*
>
> Sandy Krauss

EPILOGUE

You made it — Congratulations! I hope you have found the concepts and ideas on the preceding pages valuable and encouraging. The next step is to continue to hold on to your commitment to grow, to nurture yourself and to never give up on your dreams.

As you move forward on your journey, remember what you have learned from *Set Yourself Free: How to Unlock the Greatness Within You* and let those thoughts be your guide.

Remember... you are worth it. Keep up the great work! I've enjoyed sharing this part of your journey with you.

Recommended Reading

I am often asked for recommendations about books that have made a difference in my life. The following pages are just some of the many books that have made a significant contribution to my growth and success.

A Return to Love by Marianne Williamson.
New York: *Harper Collins Publishers*, 1993.

Awaken the Giant Within by Anthony Robbins.
New York: FIRESIDE, 1991.

Chicken Soup for the Soul® Series
by Jack Canfield and Mark Victor Hansen.
Florida: Health Communications.

Dare to Win by Jack Canfield and Mark Victor Hansen.
California: Berkeley, 1994.

Feel the Fear and Do It Anyway by Susan Jeffers, Ph.D.
New York: Ballantine Books, 1987.

Happiness is a Choice by Barry Neil Kaufman.
New York: Ballantine Books, 1991.

How to Raise Your Self-Esteem by Nathaniel Branden.
New York: Bantam Books, 1987.

How to Win Friends & Influence People by Dale Carnegie.
New York: Simon & Schuster, Inc. Copyright 1936, 1964, 1981.

Mastery: A Technology for Excellence and Personal Evolution by Tim Piering.
California: Sun West Publishing Company, 1988.

One Day My Soul Just Opened Up by Iyanla Vanzant.
New York: Fireside Publishing, 1998.

Simple Abundance by Sarah Ban Breathnach.
New York: Warner Books, 1995.

The Aladdin Factor by Jack Canfield and Mark Victor Hansen.
New York: The Berkley Publishing Group, 1995.

The Greatest Secret in the World by Og Mandino.
New York: Frederick Fell Publishers, Inc., 1972.

The Magic of Thinking Big by David J. Schwartz, Ph.D..
New York: Simon & Schuster, Inc., 1987

The Seven Habits of Highly Effective People by Stephen Covey.
New York: Simon & Schuster, 1989.

Think and Grow Rich by Napoleon Hill.
New York: Ballantine Books, 1960.

You Can Heal Your Life by Louise Hay.
California: Hay House.

About Sandy . . .

Sandy Krauss is dedicated to helping people stay motivated as they make positive changes in their lives. As a speaker and author, Sandy presents programs on self-esteem, the psychology of success and staying motivated.

Sandy is president of two companies, Success Talks, Inc. and The Motivation Store, a mail-order and Internet-based company offering resources for motivation, inspiration, celebration and acknowledgment.

Believing the power to be successful is in every one of us, Sandy encourages us to focus on areas in our lives where we can improve and take action!

Her hobbies include traveling, backpacking and reading. Sandy lives in Cleveland, Ohio with her husband, Ted.

Order Form
(over)

Share the Greatness!
Order additional copies of
Set Yourself Free ~ How to Unlock
the Greatness Within You
for those you love.

ORDER FORM

Here's how you can share what you have learned in *Set Yourself Free: How to Unlock the Greatness Within You*.

Order this special gift for your family, friends and co-workers today.
To place your order today, call 800-784-1698 or complete and mail this Order Form.

1. *Set Yourself Free: How to Unlock the Greatness Within You* ...... $14.95 each

Order Information

Number of copies: _____ x $14.95 = _____

Shipping & Handling (see chart to right): _____

TOTAL: _____

Shipping & Handling:	
1-2 books	$3.20
3-5 books	$4.20
6-9 books	$5.20
10 or more, please call for shipping information.	

2. *Payment Information*

❏ check or money order enclosed (made payable to *Success Talks, Inc.*)

❏ Credit card information

please circle one   VISA   Master Card   Discover

Credit Card #: _____

Expiration Date: _____

Signature (required): _____

3. *Shipping Information*

name: _____

address: _____

city: _____   state: _____   zip: _____

phone:(   )_____   fax: (   )_____

email: _____

4. Mail to: Or call:
Success Talks, Inc.   1-800-784-1698
PO Box 33593
North Royalton, Ohio 44133-3593

Thank you for your order!